Poetry as Discourse

ANTONY EASTHOPE

METHUEN
London and New York

First published in 1983 by
Methuen & Co. Ltd
11 New Fetter Lane, London EC4P 4EE
Published in the USA by
Methuen & Co.
in association with Methuen, Inc.
733 Third Avenue, New York, NY 10017

Photoset by Rowland Phototypesetting Ltd
Bury St Edmunds, Suffolk
Printed in Great Britain by
Richard Clay (The Chaucer Press)
Bungay, Suffolk

British Library Cataloguing in Publication Data

Easthope, Antony
Poetry as discourse.—(New accents)
1. Poetry—History and criticism
I. Title II. Series
809.1 PN1111

ISBN 0-416-32720-6
ISBN 0-416-32730-3 Pbk

Library of Congress Cataloging in Publication Data

Easthope, Antony.
Poetry as discourse.
(New accents)
Bibliography: p.
Includes index.
1. English poetry—History and criticism.
2. Discourse analysis, Literary. 3. Poetry.
I. Title II. Series: New accents (Methuen & Co.)
PR508.D57E2 1983 808.1'0141 82-18856

ISBN 0-416-32720-6
ISBN 0-416-32730-3 (pbk.)

Contents

General editor's preface

It is easy to see that we are living in a time of rapid and radical social change. It is much less easy to grasp the fact that such change will inevitably affect the nature of those academic disciplines that both reflect our society and help to shape it.

Yet this is nowhere more apparent than in the central field of what may, in general terms, be called literary studies. Here, among large numbers of students at all levels of education, the erosion of the assumptions and presuppositions that support the literary disciplines in their conventional form has proved fundamental. Modes and categories inherited from the past no longer seem to fit the reality experienced by a new generation.

New Accents is intended as a positive response to the initiative offered by such a situation. Each volume in the series will seek to encourage rather than resist the process of change, to stretch rather than reinforce the boundaries that currently define literature and its academic study.

Some important areas of interest immediately present themselves. In various parts of the world, new methods of analysis have been developed whose conclusions reveal the limitations of the Anglo-American outlook we inherit. New concepts of literary forms and modes have been proposed; new notions of the nature of literature itself, and of how it communicates, are current; new views of literature's role in relation to society flourish. *New Accents* will aim to expound and comment upon the most notable of these.

In the broad field of the study of human communication, more and more emphasis has been placed upon the nature and function of the new electronic media. *New Accents* will try to identify and discuss the challenge these offer to our traditional modes of critical response.

The same interest in communication suggests that the series should also concern itself with those wider anthropological and sociological areas of investigation which have begun to involve scrutiny of the nature of art itself and of its relation to our whole way of life. And this will ultimately require attention to be focused on some of those activities which in our society have hitherto been excluded from the prestigious realms of Culture. The disturbing realignment of values involved and the disconcerting nature of the pressures that work to bring it about both constitute areas that *New Accents* will seek to explore.

Finally, as its title suggests, one aspect of *New Accents* will be firmly located in contemporary approaches to language, and a continuing concern of the series will be to examine the extent to which relevant branches of linguistic studies can illuminate specific literary areas. The volumes with this particular interest will nevertheless presume no prior technical knowledge on the part of their readers, and will aim to rehearse the linguistics appropriate to the matter in hand, rather than to embark on general theoretical matters.

Each volume in the series will attempt an objective exposition of significant developments in its field up to the present as well as an account of its author's own views of the matter. Each will culminate in an informative bibliography as a guide to further study. And while each will be primarily concerned with matters relevant to its own specific interests, we can hope that a kind of conversation will be heard to develop between them: one whose accents may perhaps suggest the distinctive discourse of the future.

TERENCE HAWKES

Acknowledgements

As the main contribution to this book I should like to acknowledge the help I have had from working with the Manchester Reading Group of the Society for Education in Film and Television, especially Marie-Noëlle Lamy, Rob Lapsley, John O. Thompson and Michael Westlake. I should also like to thank Terence Hawkes, who encouraged the idea of the book from the start and continued to give valuable criticism during its development. Among others from whom I have learned about poetry, both through agreement and disagreement, are Catherine Belsey, Margaret Beetham, Andrew Collier, Elspeth Graham, Alf Louvre, Brian Maidment and Jeffrey Wainwright. Of course what goes into a book is one thing and what comes out is another.

I am grateful to Derek Attridge for the loan of a copy of *The Rhythms of English Poetry* before its publication; to David Crystal for answering a request for information with the information and the loan of a book; and also to my colleagues in the Department of English and History at Manchester Polytechnic, who supported my application for study leave.

Chapter 4 is revised and expanded from an essay first published in *New Literary History*. In an earlier form sections of Chapters 3 and 8 appeared in the *Proceedings* of the Essex Sociology of Literature Conference for 1980 and 1981.

The author and publishers would like to thank the following for their permission to reproduce copyright material: ATV Music Ltd for 'Tutti Frutti' by Richard Penniman and Dorothy Labostrie; Faber & Faber Ltd and Harcourt Brace Jovanovich, Inc. for 'Morning at the window' from *Collected Poems 1909–1962* by T. S. Eliot (in the US copyright 1936 by Harcourt Brace Jovanovich, Inc.; copyright © 1963, 1964 by T. S. Eliot); Faber & Faber Ltd and New Directions Publishing Corporation for 'In a station of the Metro' from (in the UK) *Collected Shorter Poems* by Ezra Pound, and (in the US) *Personae* by Ezra Pound © 1926 Ezra Pound; and for 71 and 4 lines from 'Canto 84' from *The Cantos of Ezra Pound* by Ezra Pound (in the US © 1948 Ezra Pound).

Part I
A theory of discourse

I

Discourse as language

My words are things before they
become words, and they become things
again when they do

Michael Westlake,
One Zero and the Night Controller

In modern society we are surrounded by poetry more than we realize. In unofficial forms there are the nursery rhymes and skipping games learned by children, forgotten, then often relearned by them later from their own children. Via the transistor radio and records pop music pervades the environment; its lyrics are written in lines, they invariably rhyme, and so by any neutral definition, they are a form of poetry. Unofficial poetry is used in advertising, on toilet walls, in football chants:

Georgie, Georgie, Georgie Best!
Georgie! $\wedge$ Georgie Best!   ($\wedge$ = miss a beat)

and at political demonstrations:

Black and white
Unite and fight!

In 'official' forms there is poetry in church and in the Bible:

A bundle of myrrh is my wellbeloved unto me;
He shall lie all night betwixt my breasts.
(Song of Solomon, I, 13)

However, the main official form of poetry, promoted in schools and universities, is that of the high cultural tradition from the

Renaissance to the present day. It is this canonical tradition that I shall be mainly concerned with here. I will argue that it may be better understood as a form of discourse.

Conventional literary theory

There is already a way of interpreting poetry put forward in conventional literary criticism, though with rather different emphases in Britain and America. The British version can be typified by a review of a National Theatre performance that appeared in *The Sunday Times*. For the performance an actor read 50 of Shakespeare's sonnets. The poetry was seen as a form of the author's presence:

> It is almost as if Shakespeare himself were talking to you from that pool of light . . . the experience has been like having a glimpse into Shakespeare's soul . . . He speaks nakedly as 'I' for the only time. (*The Sunday Times*, 8 June 1980, p. 33)

Although a piece of journalism, the review draws on a number of literary critics who have written on Shakespeare's sonnets (including W. H. Auden, Stephen Booth and Martin Seymour-Smith). Its attitudes correspond to much that can be found elsewhere in British criticism of poetry. For example, in the introduction to an edition of Donne's *Songs and Sonets*, Helen Gardner identifies the poetry with 'the personality of Donne' (1965, p. xviii) and claims it has 'the dramatic intensity of present experience' (p. xix). F. R. Leavis, in an earlier account, defines poetry in terms of the poet:

> He is a poet because his interest in his experience is not separable from his interest in words; because, that is, of his habit of seeking by the evocative use of words to sharpen his awareness of his ways of feeling, so making these communicable. And poetry can communicate the actual quality of experience with a subtlety and precision unapproachable by any other means. (1972, p. 17)

Literary criticism in Britain is not always as explicit about its assumptions as this. Yet other examples of the same idea of poetry could easily be brought forward. Poetry expresses experience; experience gives access to personality, and so poetry leads us to personality. In poetry 'the actual quality of experience' is communicated; reading Donne is a 'present experience', and so poetry is to be read in search of 'the personality of Donne' or of a Shakespeare who 'speaks nakedly as "I"'. A simple point about this notion, but one still worth making as a preliminary, is that Shakespeare the historical author died in 1616, and John Donne, Dean of St Paul's, died in 1631. Whatever ghost walks the boards of the National Theatre or haunts the study of a reader of *Songs and Sonets* has stepped from the pages of a text, a script or book, held by a twentieth-century hand. This in essence is the theme of *Poetry as Discourse*.

Because the influence of T. S. Eliot and I. A. Richards has been stronger there, the conventional American conception of poetry is somewhat different, at least on first inspection. Eliot's essay 'Tradition and the Individual Talent' says that honest criticism should be directed 'not upon the poet but upon the poetry' (1966, p. 17). The American New Critics took up this emphasis, particularly in relation to poetry, and its consequences can be seen clearly in the essay on 'The Intentional Fallacy' by W. K. Wimsatt and Monroe C. Beardsley. Against the view that poetry expresses the author's experience and intention they pronounce:

> The poem is not the critic's own and not the author's (it is detached from the author at birth and goes about the world beyond his power to intend about it or control it). The poem belongs to the public. It is embodied in language, the peculiar possession of the public, and it is about the human being, an object of public knowledge. (1970, p. 5)

So the author, if he (*sic*) comes into the poem at all, only does so 'by an act of biographical inference' (p. 5) since the poem is self-sufficient without him. The poem is like 'a machine' – it works 'through its *meaning*' and meaning inheres in words, since language is in public ownership. From this American account there emerges what is now a familiar figure in literary criticism on both sides of the Atlantic: the poem 'out there', an object, a 'verbal icon', the 'meaning expressed by the poem itself' (ibid., p. 87), fixed eternally as 'the words on the page'. The difficulty is that no such object, a poem with a single fixed or univocal meaning, exists. A poem constantly changes its meanings as it is read and re-read.

For this reason, as Catherine Belsey has shown very clearly in *Critical Practice*, an earlier volume in this series, New Criticism threw the author out of the front door only to sneak him or her in round the back. The author's intention was needed to fix in place, to guarantee, an univocal meaning for 'the words on the page', even if in the American emphasis this guarantee was available only at a remove. What survives from New Criticism is 'a kind of implicit intentionalism, a quest for what it *appeared* the author had had in mind on the evidence of the text itself' (Belsey 1980, p. 16). Wimsatt and Beardsley had left open this loophole: 'If the poet succeeded in doing it, then the poem itself shows what he was trying to do' (Wimsatt 1970, p. 4). On this basis it becomes possible to distinguish the 'implied author', the author implied by the poem, from the actual historical author. And on this basis it becomes possible to equate them again by treating the implied author as a mask worn by the historical author. In *The Rhetoric of Fiction* Wayne C. Booth introduces the term 'implied author' by saying that this is how the historical author 'creates . . . an implied version of "himself"' (1961, p. 70). Thus re-routed, the poem can once again be fixed in place as expression of the author's experience and intention, and read in terms of personality and presence.

Conventional literary criticism in Britain and America can be contrasted as follows: in Britain it moves directly from the poem to the author's experience while in America it moves indirectly from the poem as artefact to the author who made it as a version of himself or herself. Both positions have recourse to authorial intention for the same reason: to try to fix the poem in terms of a univocal meaning given, once and for all, by 'the words on the page'. This formulation sounds very confident but it cannot stand up to interrogation by any linguistics which takes account of the work of Ferdinand de Saussure. Saussure's distinction between signifier and signified, between the *sound image* (the shaped, material sound of the word) and *concept* (the meaning of the word), applies to all words, and so can be applied to these 'words on the page' of the poem. The question which then arises is: are these words on the page signifiers or signifieds? Clearly the assumption silently invoked by the usual way the phrase is used is that 'on the page' the signifieds are forever fixed on to their signifiers and the meaning of the poem is forever attached to the sounds represented there. This is not the case. The signifiers of a text such as a poem do have a material identity (these signifiers and not others) defined within the structure of signifiers in a given language, as Saussure shows. Further, they can have a physical identity fixed on the page by means of a writing system which aims to represent phonetic correspondence with the sound. But the signifieds are *not* fixed and cannot be so fixed. Any text, especially one such as a poem, is constantly read and re-read in different ways – by different people, by the same people at different times in their lives, by different people at different periods in history.

The meaning of a text is always produced in a process of reading. It is in order to bring a necessary stability to this process that conventional criticism of poetry treats the poem in relation to the supposed intentions and personality of the author. In so doing it is in fact reading poetry not simply as language but with the implicit assumption that it is a certain kind of discourse. I intend to make fully explicit the idea that poetry is to be read as discourse and also propose a conception of discourse that gives a better understanding of poetry than that assumed in conventional criticism. A major reason why the theory of discourse I shall put forward ought to be preferred is that it can explain the author as product or effect of the text, whereas conventional criticism accepts the notion of the author as unquestionable and pre-given in order to be able to define how the text should be read.

Language and discourse

Saussure distinguishes between *langue* and *parole*, between the system of a language, and any act of individual utterance that takes place within it. *Parole* depends upon *langue* in that an individual utterance can only be an instance of the system which makes it possible – I cannot speak in English without making use of the sounds and syntax of English. A poem obviously is an example of *parole*, an utterance constructed according to and within the system of a language. But then so is any utterance in that language, not just a poem. To understand what is specific to poetry we need to distinguish between language and discourse.

Linguistics, the science which takes language as its object, can show how an utterance takes its place in the system of language at levels up to and including the sentence. It cannot show how and why one sentence connects with another into a cohesive whole: this is a matter of discourse. The term *discourse* and the distinction between it and language is not modern. In 1776 the British rhetorician George Campbell in his *Philosophy of Rhetoric* pointed out that 'Syntax regards only the composition of many words into one sentence; style, at the same time that it attends to this, regards further the composition of many sentences into one discourse' (cited in Hendricks 1976, p. 32). A revised and updated expression of the distinction is given by Emile Benveniste as follows:

> Phonemes, morphemes and words (lexemes) can be counted; there is a finite number of them. Not so with sentences. Phonemes, morphemes and words (lexemes) have a distribution at their respective levels and a use at higher levels. Sentences have neither distribution nor use . . . with the sentence we leave the domain of language as a system of signs and enter into another universe . . . whose expression is discourse (Benveniste 1971, pp. 109–10)

Shakespeare's 'Sonnet 73' contains four sentences. Each is an instance of sentence structure in Modern English. The cohesion of these four sentences together is the province of discourse.

Discourse, then, is a term which specifies the way that sentences form a consecutive order, take part in a whole which is homogeneous as well as heterogeneous. And just as sentences join together in discourse to make up an individual text, so texts themselves join others in a larger discourse. In fact, the way in which Eliot in his famous essay describes the relation between tradition and the individual poem can be interpreted as an accurate account of how texts are ordered in relation to each other as discourse. As Eliot says:

> The existing monuments form an ideal order among themselves, which is modified by the introduction of the new (the really new) work of art among them. The existing order is

complete before the new work arrives; for order to persist after the supervention of novelty, the *whole* existing order must be, if ever so slightly, altered; and so the relations, proportions, values of each work of art toward the whole are readjusted; and this is conformity between the old and the new. (1966, p. 15)

This is advanced as an account of aesthetic discourse in general. But it can be accepted as an analysis of the cohesion of a discourse, including a particular poetic discourse such as that of English poetry since the Renaissance. Each additional text both repeats the discourse and differs from it, each is a term which conforms to the discourse but (however slightly) transforms it. Of course a poem has to be understood in language (how else?) but it has to be grasped also as an instance of a poetic discourse, part of an autonomy in which the monuments form an 'order among themselves'. The only word of Eliot's account I shall disagree with (in Chapter 2) is the word 'ideal'. And I shall reconsider Eliot's essay with reference to Modernism in Chapter 9.

There is already in existence a conventional theory of discourse analysis. Since this is not the one to be set to work in this book, it will be discussed briefly in order to be rejected. Conventional discourse analysis brings together work from a number of different areas, including linguistics and philosophy. It has found a philosophic underpinning in the work of J. L. Austin, especially in his *How to do Things with Words* (1962). In this tradition the analysis of discourse consists particularly of a careful description of different discourses on the general assumption that the production of discourse is a rule-governed activity and that these rules, like those of syntax or of chess, generate specific examples. Although this summary is too broad and there are important differences of emphasis within conventional discourse analysis, I shall not attempt to distinguish these since the tradition rests on a central assumption, one so deeply held that it is rarely made explicit for comment and criticism: it is that language and with it discourse is a matter of communication:

(a) 'But a piece of language use, literary or otherwise, is not only an exemplification of linguistic categories . . . but is also a piece of *communication*, a discourse of one kind or another'. (my italics) (Widdowson, 'Literature as Discourse' in *Stylistics and the Teaching of Literature* (1975), p. 27)

(b) 'While all linguists would agree that *human communication* must be described in terms of at least three levels – meaning, form and substance, or *discourse*, *syntax* and *phonology* – there are disagreements over the boundaries of linguistics.' (Coulthard, *An Introduction to Discourse Analysis* (1977), p. 1)

(c) 'The processes discussed in the last few sections demonstrate that a good deal of what gets *communicated* through language is "unspoken" in the sense that it involves conveying meanings other than or in addition to the literal meaning of what is said. The importance of this fact emerges particularly clearly in the analysis of discourse.' (my italics) (Traugott and Pratt, 'Analysing Discourse' in *Linguistics for Students of Literature* (1980), p. 241)

Briefly stated, the difficulty here is simple and fundamental. To identify language and so discourse with communication operates a kind of synecdoche. It gives us the part for the whole. Communication, *one* major effect of discourse, is generalized and made into a definition of discourse as a whole.

The classic diagram of language as communication is offered by Jakobson. His 'concise survey of the constitutive factors in any speech event, in any act of verbal communication' specifies six factors. Three ('CONTEXT', 'CONTACT', 'CODE') function as 'means' by which the act of communication takes place and three define the event itself, 'The ADDRESSER sends a MESSAGE to the ADDRESSEE' (Jakobson 1960, p. 353). All these factors are schematized as follows:

CONTEXT
MESSAGE
ADDRESSER-------------------------ADDRESSEE
CONTACT
CODE

There are two necessary conditions for this model. One is that language should be conceived as a more or less transparent 'medium' for communication. The other is that the subject, whether as 'addresser' or 'addressee', should be assumed to be a self-sufficient 'individual', given prior to language, standing outside language, and so able to intend and communicate a message *through* it. It is notable that conventional discourse theory conceives the 'individual' in very much the same way as conventional literary criticism conceives the poet. Leavis's poet, for instance, stood outside language and took an interest in words, used language but was in no sense 'used' by it. This assumption is to be a central topic in Chapter 3 and so fuller discussion will be left until there. Here the main argument against the conventional notion of discourse is that language is inherently not transparent, not a merely neutral vehicle for communication, and that communication is one special effect of language. In drawing on Saussure and Derrida to suggest that language is not inherently transparent I shall aim to demonstrate that discourse is linguistically determined, in that it follows the laws of its own material nature, its *materiality*.

'The ADDRESSER sends a MESSAGE to the ADDRESSEE' (Jakobson); 'communicated through language . . . conveying meanings' (Traugott and Pratt): there are metaphors here asking to be spelt out. Thus, in this view, language is a vehicle like one for transporting coal. Someone in Merthyr Tydfil (the addresser) sends coal to someone else in Cardiff (the addressee). The coal is conveyed in coal trucks. Possibly on the way some of the content of the trucks is lost (stolen by the unemployed) or added to (bird-droppings) but essentially what was put in by the addresser is tipped out at the other end by the addressee. The trucks are conceived as merely a passive means perfectly adapted to their end and having in themselves no more effect on the coal than a pane of glass has on the light waves which pass through it.

The inadequacy of this model can be seen if it is consistently transposed into Saussurean terms, specifically those of the distinction between signifier and signified. Thus, the message communicated (the coal) is the signified and the means of communication (the truck) is the signifier. There are two related features of the signifier which destroy the theory of language as transparent communication. First, the theory assumes that signifiers are naturally adapted to convey signifieds just as coal trucks are to carrying coal (they would be of no use for flour or whisky by the gallon). But the Saussurean conception stresses that the relation between signifier and signified is by nature arbitrary. The signifier, consisting of sound, is ineluctably physical and so is of an entirely different order from meaning and the signified. Second, the conventional theory denies that signifiers have any autonomy, any force or weight of their own. But again Saussure shows that they do, as can be understood most readily if the signifier is considered at the level of the phoneme, the smallest unit of sound systematized in a given language. The phoneme /p/ works because in Modern English it is opposed to /b/, so that /pig/ is contrasted with /big/. So all the phonemes of a language define each other in a system of mutual differentiation: 'Phonemes are characterized not, as one might think, by their own positive quality but simply by the fact that they are distinct. Phonemes are above all else opposing, relative, and negative entities' (Saussure 1959, p. 119). Subsequent work by Jakobson and Halle has shown that the kinds of phonemic opposition in all the known languages in the world 'amount to twelve oppositions, out of which each language makes its own selection' (1956, p. 29). As phonemes, signifiers relate in the first place to *each other*, and not to any signified. They thus have a material force and organization of their own. What differentiates /big/ from /pig/ is the sound, not the intention of the speaker. The implication for a theory of language as transparent communication should be clear. If signifiers have an autonomy and determining action of their own, the signifier is not transparent in respect of the signified, not merely a passive means of communication. Of course the signifier can be treated as if it were transparent, merely a means to an end, but this is one use of language in a particular discursive form and cannot be equated with the nature of language in general. Saussure speaks of language as a 'social fact' (1959, p. 113) – the signifier is a fact, physically and materially *there* prior to the intention of any individual who wants to communicate. Since there can be no signified without a signifier, the signifier should be envisaged as the level or order of language preceding the signified rather than as subordinate to it. 'Words are things before they become words, and they become things again when they do.'

The precedence of the signifier

The work of Jacques Derrida can be understood as a critique of the notion of language as communication and as an assertion of the materiality of all discourse. Derrida's *Of Grammatology* begins by recalling the way that the western tradition has always valued speech as primary and writing as secondary to it. For example, according to Aristotle in *De Interpretatione* 'spoken words (ta en tē phonē) are the symbols of mental experience (pathēmata tes psychēs) and written words are the symbols of spoken words' because it is supposed that 'the voice, producer *of the first symbols*, has a relationship of essential and immediate proximity with the mind' (Derrida 1976, p. 11). Mind expresses meaning (the signified) almost but not quite transparently through words (the signifier), and so writing is disparaged as derivative, merely a technical addition of the written signifier to the spoken one: 'writing, the letter, the sensible inscription, has always been considered by western tradition as the body and matter external to the spirit, to breath, to speech and to the logos' (ibid., p. 35). Derrida gives the term *logocentrism* to the view that speech is the original source of meaning and the location of its full presence. He questions everything such logocentrism implies, and argues that, far from standing in an accidental relation to the 'essence' of language, writing is evidence of a materiality integral to language itself.

The implications of this position for a notion of discourse as communication – 'the addresser sends a message to the addressee' – are cogently and lucidly developed by Derrida in an essay, 'Signature Event Context'. This specifically criticizes the work of Austin, which is generally used to support conventional discourse theory. The essay points out that writing operates in the absence of the addressee – 'one writes in order to communicate something to those who are absent' (Derrida 1977, p. 177). Further, what holds for the addressee holds also for the addresser; the original writer and his or her reader may both be absent or dead but it is in the nature of writing for it to be still readable by others. This is because writing is 'a sort of machine':

> A written sign . . . is a mark that subsists, one which does not

> exhaust itself in the moment of its inscription and which can give rise to an iteration in the absence and beyond the presence of the empirically determined subject who, in a given context, has emitted or produced it. (ibid., pp. 181–2)

So far the argument has hardly departed from common sense, and it is what happens next with the notion of writing as mechanical ('a sort of machine') that undermines traditional views. For if the written sign is a mark that can be reproduced or read or iterated apart from its 'original' context, it is because of the material operation of language in general, of which writing is only an *illustration*. The written – what Derrida terms the *graphematic* feature – is not accidental to language but central to its very structure, and so manifest in speech *as well as* in writing. The graphematic is present not only in the readings of a text which it makes possible beyond its so-called 'original' or 'real' context but even in the 'original' context itself:

> Every sign, linguistic, or non-linguistic, spoken or written . . . can be *cited*, put between quotation marks; but in so doing it can break with every given context, engendering an infinity of new contexts in a manner which is absolutely illimitable. This does not imply that the mark is valid outside of a context, but on the contrary that there are only contexts without any center or absolute anchoring. (ibid., pp. 185–6)

The notion of an original context as source of meaning is replaced by the idea of a variety of potential contexts of which the so-called original is only one. This is substantiated in Derrida's discussion of language as a form of conscious intention. Traditionally speech has been given priority over writing because the voice apparently expresses the mind without mediation; the conscious intention of the speaker has been held to govern the whole of the speech act. But if language is admitted to be a sort of machine, then the graphematic will always 'interpose' between a writer's conscious intention and any reception of this text – more than interpose, it will be a condition of the text: 'the category of intention will not disappear; it will have its place, but from that place it will no longer be able to govern the entire scene and system of utterance' (ibid., p. 192). This holds for both speech and writing. Because of the graphematic, the ineluctable materiality of language, no text can ever be fully permeated by conscious intention – the text will always mean for its readers something other than it means for its author. In every text, written or spoken, read silently or performed aloud, there will always be some 'gap' between intention and reading. Derrida refers to this gap as *différance*, and defines it by saying 'the irreducible absence of intention or attendance to the performative utterance, the most "event-ridden" utterance there is, is what authorizes me . . . to posit the general graphematic structure of every "communication"' (ibid., pp. 192–3). (Oral poetry is particularly 'event-ridden', since it is performed, and there will be reference back to Derrida's argument during discussion of the ballad in chapter 5.)

Because of the signifier and because of what Derrida defines as the graphematic, all discourse must be understood as determined linguistically, according to the laws of its own materiality. Poetry is an extreme instance of this determination, as can be understood if we compare Derrida's account with Jakobson's and the definition he gives in the rest of that essay. According to Jakobson, in language there is always a signifier but in prose (non-poetic discourse) the signifier is to be disregarded in favour of the signified, the message communicated. He takes this as the norm of language. Then the 'poetic function' is defined as a specialized use of language in which the signifier intensifies the message. A political slogan such as 'I like Ike' is preferable to (say) 'Ike for me' or even 'I admire Ike' because the use of the signifier, the three monosyllablic diphthongs, 'reinforces' the message (Jakobson 1960, p. 357). Poetry aims to maximize this effect, to bring the signifier into a reinforcing relation with the signified, so giving the poetic message a quality of 'reification' able to convert it 'into an enduring thing' (ibid., p. 371). Derrida's account of language can be understood as an inversion of Jakobson's. For Jakobson communication *through* the supposed transparency of language is normal, while poetry is a specialized usage which, by trying to make the signifier at one with the signified, presents language as a 'thing'. In Derrida *all* language is characterized by its reification or 'thingness'; and it would follow that prose is a specialized use of language. It is possible, however, to accept that the signifier precedes the signified in all language (so rejecting the belief that communication is the norm of language) while still endorsing much of Jakobson's account of poetry.

Poetry can be distinguished from prose not by the presence of the signifier but by the special use it makes of the signifier in patterns of repetition and condensation, patterns such as that Jakobson discovers in 'I like Ike'. Relative to other discourses, poetry thus draws attention to – or *foregrounds* – the signifier, as Mukařovský argues in his essay 'Standard Language and Poetic Language', where he states that 'the function of poetic language consists in the maximum foregrounding of the utterance' (1964, p. 19). This feature helps to describe and explain three general effects of poetry. First, as Mukařovský goes on to show, foregrounding in poetry has the effect of 'pushing communication into the background as the objective of expression' and asserting that language is 'being used for its own sake' (ibid., p. 19). Through repetition in the signifier, poetry signals that it is to be read as a fictional discourse. Second, such repetition serves to mark poetry as separate from prose. It contributes to an effect noted by Ruth Finnegan in an almost comprehensive survey of oral poetry round the world, namely 'the way in which a poem is, as it were, italicized, set apart from everyday life and language' (1977, p. 25). Poetry shares these two qualities with other forms of aesthetic discourse, such as drama and the novel.

A third quality is specific to poetry. Poetry is organized into lines and, as will be discussed further in chapter 4, line organization or metre takes place mainly – though not exclusively – on the basis of phonetic parallelism, the repetition of sound line by line through the poem. This repetition must promote other kinds of repetition in poetry, phonetic, syntactic and semantic. So, in several ways, one of which is entirely specific to it, poetry contains repetitions in the signifier which thus work to foreground the signifier. This feature can stand as a definition of poetry.

It is useful and necessary to have some general sense of what poetry is, though any definition at this level remains only abstract. All discourse, including a poetic discourse, occurs only in specific local and national forms. The English high cultural poetic tradition from the Renaissance to the twentieth century is one historical discourse. And in so far as discourse is always historical – *a* discourse – it is determined not just materially but at the same time ideologically, as will be argued in Chapter 2.

Saussure distinguishes between the *sound image* or signifier and the *concept* or signified. Reference, how and in what ways a signified may refer to a reality lying beyond it, is another matter altogether. The question of reference is philosophically fraught and not one I need to enter into here except to make two assertions relevant to poetry and the study of it. First, as Mukařovský suggests, in literature language is 'used for its own sake' and so poetry is not to be treated as a discourse which refers to a reality. As Sidney says, 'the poet . . . nothing affirms, and therefore never lieth' (1947, p. 33); as Wittgenstein says, 'Do not forget that a poem, even though it is composed in the language of information is not used in the language-game of giving information' (cited in Forrest-Thomson 1978, p. x). The language of a poem may aim for transparency but this does not make a poem referential. Transparency, a certain relation of signifier and signified, is not the same thing as reference, which is a relation between the signified and reality. Second, in all discourse the signifier precedes the signified and no discourse is by nature transparent. But this fact does not preclude there being a discourse which gives knowledge by referring to a reality. It does mean that a discourse providing such knowledge depends upon the reader being positioned so as to read the discourse as transparent and treat it as referential. On this basis the study of poetry can give knowledge of poetry by referring to it accurately.

The account of discourse proposed by this book is intended to apply to all discourses. However, the theory is especially appropriate for the analysis of poetry since a poetic discourse is distinguishable from other, non-poetic discourses by the way it accords precedence to the signifier. To theorize poetry as a discourse entails that attention will not be focused on individual texts or even several texts grouped as the work of a single author. Instead, texts and passages will be looked at in terms of the discourse they each participate in and exemplify. *Poetry as Discourse* aims to be a work of *formalism* rather than *contentism*. It is written in the belief that poetry always occurs as a specific material discourse. Accordingly, the more closely analysis is directed at the signifier (rather than the signified) and at the level of discourse (rather than that of the single text), the more likely it is to produce a systematic understanding and accurate knowledge of what it discusses.

2
Discourse as ideology

A little formalism turns one away from History . . . a lot brings one back to it

Roland Barthes,
Mythologies

The relative autonomy of a poetic discourse

In assuming that poetry is defined only by repetition and condensation of the signifier, Jakobson's essay conforms to the old Russian Formalist tradition. But it is also the case that poetry is always *a* poetic discourse and so exhibits possibilities and limits that are historical. Discourse, in Saussure's phrase, is a social *fact* and also a *social* fact: linguistic determination simultaneously involves ideological determination. Eliot's conclusion that the 'monuments form an ideal order among themselves' is correct in affirming the self-consistency of a poetic discourse. But it is mistaken to conceive this autonomy as ideal, transcendental and absolute rather than material, historical and relative.

In advocating that literary criticism 'should be able to give some intelligible account of the relation of literature to the social order', Graham Hough has recognized that this 'requires some application of Marxism' (1970, p. 57). In the classic Marxist statement of this relationship: 'the economic structure of society' is a base, 'the real foundation' on which 'rises a legal and political superstructure'. 'Aesthetic forms' (including poetry) are some of the 'ideological forms' of 'social consciousness' corresponding to and determined by the economic structure at the base (Marx and Engels 1950, I, pp. 328–9). Poetry as an ideological form is not identical with the economic base, for if it were it would not be visible as something separate from it. Although in every epoch 'the ruling ideas are nothing more than the ideal expression of the dominant material relationships' (Marx and Engels 1970, p. 64), they are nothing less than them either, an 'ideal' and therefore to some extent autonomous expression:

> each new class which puts itself in the place of one ruling before it, is compelled, merely in order to carry through its aim, to represent its interest as the common interest of all the members of society, that is, expressed in ideal form: it has to give its ideas the form of universality, and represent them as the only rational, universally valid ones. (ibid., p. 65–6)

Ideology does not 'reflect' the economic structure of society. For these 'ideas' to be effective *as ideology* they have to expand into 'the form of universality' in an attempt to fill all the available intellectual 'space'. In 'form' and 'content' ideology has an independence, though this very independence is related back to class interest. Ideology must operate as ideology and not something else. The autonomy of ideology, which includes of course the autonomy of literary forms and poetry, can be understood through some qualifications and explanations given by Engels to the theory of base and superstructure. Engels writes (in letters to J. Bloch and C. Schmidt) that the 'production and reproduction of real life' is 'the *ultimately* determining element in history' and that it finally asserts itself through 'interaction' with the political and ideological elements of the superstructure (Marx and Engels, 1950, II, p. 443). So, for example, the state as a political power has a 'relative independence' from economic conditions (ibid., p. 447), a concept which is given further definition with reference to law as a superstructural form. In a modern state a code of law must be both an expression of general economic conditions (and so relative to the base) but it must also 'be an *internally coherent* expression which does not, owing to inner contradictions, reduce itself to nought' (ibid., p. 448).

This account has direct implications for the understanding of poetry's relation to history, that is, for the notion of a poetic discourse as ideological. If the state has a 'relative independence' and law both relates to society and operates as an 'internally coherent expression' as law, then poetry also can be seen as fulfilling a double obligation – to its historical position and to its own 'nature' as poetry. In the emphasis given to Engels's ideas in the reworking of them by the French Marxist Louis Althusser, poetry would be a specific instance of ideological *practice*, defined by its relative autonomy.

In the 1930s there were a number of books in the Marxist tradition which reduced poetry to an all but direct expression of the economic structure. For example Christopher Caudwell's *Illusion and Reality* tries to demonstrate that the tight closure of the eighteenth-century heroic couplet was determined by contemporary import controls (1946, pp. 46–8). What is wrong with this is its assumption that the social formation is some kind of organic unity such that a change in one part (customs duties) affected every other part (including line endings in poetry). In the Althusserian conception, society is a *decentred structure in dominance.* It is *decentred* because it consists of three main practices (economic, political, ideological), each of which is autonomous but also a necessary though not sufficient condition for the others: none of them, in short, is central. It is a structure *in dominance* because economic practice ultimately determines which of the other practices is dominant at any one time. (This is a drastically abbreviated account, and a fuller one is given by Tony Bennett in *Formalism and Marxism*, an earlier volume of the present series, 1979, pp. 36–43.) In a way fully compatible with the writings of Marx and Engels, Althusser makes it possible to conceive poetry as both autonomous and historically relative. On one side poetry is a distinct and concrete practice with its own independence, conforming to its own laws and effects, an order formed by the 'monuments' among themselves. On the other, and at the same time, poetry is always *a* poetic discourse, part of a social formation defined historically. The two aspects form a simultaneity which Andrew Collier has summarized as follows:

> For Marx, a social formation is a structure . . . which determines the social nature of its elements, *and* the contradictions between them. Its elements double as material beings subject to the laws of their own material nature, and as terms of social

relations in which they occupy definite roles generated by the structure. (Collier 1979, III, p. 77)

On this showing poetry, as an element of a social formation, is subject both to the laws of its own material nature *and* is a term in social relations. In other words, what makes poetry poetry is what makes poetry ideological.

Materialism and poetry

Althusser's work rephrased the Marxist concept of relative autonomy, stressing the 'internally coherent' laws of any practice. In the wake of this it became clear that different discourses and their means of representation also had their own autonomy, and this was acknowledged when they came to be referred to as *signifying practices* (see Heath 1974, p. 120). But to recognize this autonomy raises the problem of the relation between ideological practice and signifying practice, between 'the ideological' and 'the aesthetic'. It is a problem constantly addressed in Terry Eagleton's book, *Criticism and Ideology* (1976). The difficulty is that the distinction corresponds to that between 'content' and 'form', and is founded on the view that the text is (however indirectly) transparent and able to reflect or represent something outside itself, the 'something' in this case being ideology.

But 'content' and 'form' cannot be separated,whether as ideological practice and signifying practice, or as the ideological and the aesthetic. The refutation of this position once again lies in the fact of the precedence of the signifier. Signifieds, whether as meanings 'on the page' or as ideology, are simply not to be found lying around apart from their signifiers. Signifiers, on the other hand, are to be found all over the place, but they have their own determining action and have to be put to work in a process of reading in order to bring a signified into existence. As signified, ideology does not occur except in the form of specific discourses (Hollywood film, television news, Parliamentary debate, etc.). It does not exist 'in general', capable of being communicated transparently through discourse, but rather occurs only in specific discourses, dependent on the specific activity of specific means of representation for its production. The means of representation is not a neutral vehicle that could equally be used to convey some other ideological signified but is already 'shaped' for ideology and is therefore itself ideological.

Once transparency is rejected as defining the nature of discourse, then the form/content opposition must go. Once this goes, it is no longer possible to distinguish the signified (which is ideological) from the signifier or means of representation (which is not). Ideology can no longer be ghettoized as belonging only or mainly to the signified. This view holds for all discourse – it is only more manifestly applicable to a poetic discourse because poetry is specified by condensation of the signifier. And it confers immediate advantages on the analysis of poetry, for it at once makes visible as ideological what otherwise is disregarded as merely the means of representation. Every aspect of a poetic discourse becomes available for interrogation, especially those conventionally left unproblematized as aesthetic, formal and natural.

In their means of representation all discourses are subject (in Collier's phrase) to 'the laws of their own material nature'. Film, for example, in order to be film consists of representation through the projection of recorded moving images onto a large screen to be viewed at a distance. This discriminates its 'material nature' from slide projection on the one hand (whose recorded images don't move) and television on the other (whose moving images are presented on a small screen to be viewed intimately, see Heath and Skirrow 1977, pp. 52–7). Such materiality is always historical. Discourses and their means of representation live and die within history. Film did not exist before the end of the nineteenth century, television until the 1930s. Some discursive forms have gone forever – the masque and the madrigal for example. And while they are alive, the relationship between discourses constantly changes, as for example that between film, photography and the Renaissance tradition of linear perspective in painting (see Heath 1981). A more relevant instance here is the changing relation between music and poetry in the form of song (this will be considered in Chapter 6 with reference to the Renaissance, and again in conclusion in Chapter 10).

Poetry, then, is subject to the laws of its own materiality in being written in lines, and this feature, as was argued by the Russian Formalists or Specifiers (to give them their non-

Stalinist title) is the *dominanta* of poetry, i.e. that which specifically makes it what it is. But just as poetry is always a specific poetic discourse, so line organization always takes a specific historical form, and so is ideological. In the English poetic tradition lines are organized round a single metre, iambic pentameter, and in fact the consistent use of this metre is a major contribution to the cohesion of the discourse. In Chapter 4 iambic pentameter, so basic and material in the means of representation of the discourse, will be analysed as ideological.

The second part of this book takes the view that English poetic discourse since the Renaissance is the product of history, ideologically determined. In this respect it is an epochal form, co-terminous with the capitalist mode of production and the hegemony of the bourgeoisie as the ruling class. It is therefore a *bourgeois* poetic discourse. It will be argued that the cohesion of the discourse lies not only in the use of iambic pentameter but also in a specific 'shaping' in the signifier and means of representation, a consistency in the relation of *enunciation* and *enounced* (terms to be explained in Chapter 3). To understand this, a different account of ideology is needed. Discourse has to be seen as ideological not simply because it is a historical product but because it is one which continues to 'produce' the reader who produces it through a reading in the present.

Ideology as subject position

A poetic tradition is a relatively autonomous practice, a discourse subject to both the laws of its own materiality and its place in history. It does not 'reflect' history, yet history is inscribed in it at the level of the signifier. Read thus, a poetic discourse is a *product of history*. This is one *problematic* (or structure of questions and answers) in which it can be appropriated. But since a discourse consists of language it is always the *product of a reader*, and this is a different problematic. As Barthes says, '*in the text, only the reader speaks*' (1975, p. 151, italics original), though of course this never takes place in a voluntary or unconstrained fashion, since what the reader 'speaks' is always a historical text (even if it was composed only yesterday), and since the individual reading always takes place within a practice of reading that is socially determined. A sixteenth-century sword and a sixteenth-century sonnet are both products of history. But the poem, consisting of signifiers, is produced by the reader in the present in a way the sword can never be 'produced' by a contemporary swordsperson who uses it.

These two problematics may have been distinguished by Marx in his classic statement of the relation of base and superstructure. On the one hand 'ideological forms' as part of the superstructure are products determined by the economic structure; on the other, at times of revolution conflict occurs between economic structure and political superstructure and there are 'ideological forms in which men become conscious of this conflict and fight it out' (1950, I, p. 329). The first set of forms seems to be the product of history while the second seems rather to involve those through which people *produce* their history. Certainly the distinction is clear in Marx's equally classic paragraphs on ideology and ancient Greek art. They demonstrate how Greek art is intimately dependent on Greek myth, on 'nature and the social forms already reworked in an unconsciously artistic way by the popular imagination' (1973, p. 110). Greek myth, the ideology at stake here, is a product of what Marx elsewhere describes as 'the ancient mode of production', and could not be the product of nineteenth-century industrial capitalism. Why then do the *Iliad*, the *Oresteia* and *Oedipus Tyrannus* survive? As Marx points out:

> the difficulty lies not in understanding that the Greek arts and epic are bound up with certain forms of social development. The difficulty is that they still afford us artistic pleasure and that in a certain respect they count as a norm and as an unattainable model. (ibid., p. 111)

The two problematics are distinguished here: discourse as the product of history and discourse as product of the reader in the present. In one, Greek art must be understood as inscribed by its history, in the other it is necessarily more than that history since it is produced in a modern reading.

The issue, as Stephen Heath has shown (1977), is whether discourse and language itself is to be assigned to base or superstructure, economy or ideology. The issue was debated between the Russian linguist N. Y. Marr and Stalin. Marr argued in a paper of 1928 that 'language is just as much a super-structural value as painting or the arts in general' (Heath 1977, p. 70). Stalin refused to assign language either to superstructure (since it was not the product of a given society but of the whole of human society) or to economic base (since language doesn't produce anything). Language is thus left by Stalin as

> a sort of given autonomous instrument, rather like the air we breathe; something that is just there, perfected and ready to hand for purposes of communication and expression.
>
> (ibid., p. 71)

Stalin's view is familiar. It once again attributes transparency to language, treating it as an instrument for communication which individuals simply take up and use. In preference to this, Heath urges that we should not only recognize that production takes place both in the economic structure and the superstructure of society, but in addition we should 'edge towards a conception of a *productivity* of language' (ibid., p. 71). To illustrate the general principle that production 'not only creates an object for the subject, but also a subject for the object', Marx gives the example of art, noting that 'the object of art – like every other product – creates a public which is sensitive to art and enjoys beauty' (1973, p. 92). Understood in these terms, the conception of the productivity of language points to the view that discourse produces readers as much as readers produce discourse.

To consider readers as the products of discourse also envisages discourse as ideological, though in a different sense from that in which discourse is seen as the product of history. It can be explained with reference to the Althusserian concept of ideology which defines ideology as the very form of subjectivity constituted by a social formation. Just as Saussurean linguistics asserts that the 'social fact' of language conditions individual utterance within it, so analogously historical materialism asserts that it is not human consciousness which determines life but rather people's 'social being that determines their consciousness' (Marx and Engels 1950, I, p. 329). In class society individuals can't do what they want – 'class achieves an independent existence over against the individuals' so that they 'have their position in life and their personal development assigned to them by their class' (Marx and Engels 1970, p. 82). *Capital* seeks to analyse the way capitalist society works and in so doing treats individuals 'only in so far as they are the personifications of economic categories, embodiments (German: *Träger*) of particular class-relations' (Marx 1970, p. 21). The classical Marxist tradition of social analysis had treated individuals more or less in this way, as products of society who were *Träger*, 'bearers' or 'supports' for the social position assigned to them. Althusser's more recent theory of ideology examines the question from the side of the 'individual', asking how people come to be produced and installed as 'supports' for an economic, social or ideological position.

Written partly as a result of the 'events' of May 1968 in France, Althusser's essay on Ideological State Apparatuses needs to be taken together with Hirst's critique and correction of it (see Hirst 1979, pp. 40–74). The classic base/superstructure model, or the metaphor of economic determination 'in the last instance' is in fact static, a-temporal. Althusser emphasizes that society involves not just a structure but a process in time, a process in which each practice, economic, political, ideological, is *active*. A particular social formation seeks to reproduce itself and its relations of production by producing people, not just biologically but socially, and not just in terms of skills but of attitudes. Bourgeois society must secure for the working class 'a reproduction of submission to the ruling ideology', and for the ruling class 'a reproduction of the ability to manipulate the ruling ideology correctly' (Althusser, 1977, p. 128). People are born as 'concrete individuals' although they already have positions assigned to them sexually and socially – daughter of a merchant banker, son of a car mechanic. Ideology is what makes them work as supports for these positions: 'all ideology has the function (which defines it) of "constituting" concrete individuals as subjects' (ibid., p. 160). The term 'subject' is borrowed from the legal category of 'subject in law'. It means:

> (1) a free subjectivity, a centre of initiatives, author of and responsible for its actions; (2) a subjected being, who submits to a higher authority, and is therefore stripped of all freedom except that of freely accepting his submission. (Althusser, ibid., p. 169)

The meanings are contradictory, so how can the subject be both? Althusser's answer draws on psychoanalysis and the Lacanian conception of the *imaginary*. This latter term does not mean fictional but is a technical usage which will be discussed in the next chapter. In ideology, defined as an effect of the imaginary, subjects are constituted so as to 'see' themselves as constitutive. They are produced, socially and otherwise, to 'see' themselves as free agents.

Since in this definition ideology is a condition of individual action, we cannot escape from it, not even in a future socialist society. As Catherine Belsey points out, to try to step outside ideology 'would be to refuse to act or speak, and even to make such a refusal, to say "I refuse", is to accept the condition of subjectivity' (1980, p. 62). Yet ideology in Althusser's sense has a specific form in bourgeois society. It aims to make the subject 'see' itself as a transcendental ego, an *absolutely* free agent, centre and origin of action, unproduced, given once and for all; in the words of Shakespeare's Coriolanus

> As if a man were author of himself
> And knew no other kin.
>
> (V. iii)

The transcendental ego is a role or position assigned across a range of social practices in bourgeois society: the individual, apparently in absolute and unconstrained freedom, owning the means of production or (more frequently) exchanging labour-power for wages, acting 'freely' according to or against the law, 'freely' electing political representatives, 'freely' choosing a partner in marriage. Granted that this position exists socially, the question is how does the subject internalize it, come to *live* it? How does the social mask come to be lived as though it were a face? The answer that Althusser draws from Lacan is that the subject is produced as a subject *in language and in discourse* so as to 'work' in that position.

Two kinds of such subject position can be contrasted, one absolute, one relative. For the absolute position the subject is produced in discourse so as to deny that it is produced at all, to 'see' itself only as the transcendental ego. For a relative position the subject is produced with some degree of recognition that it *is* so produced, that the ego is determined by forces beyond itself on which it is dependent. The distinction enables the ideological effect of a discourse – *including a poetic discourse* – to be accurately described and assessed. Bourgeois forms of discourse will aim to provide an absolute position for the subject, others a relative position. But now that the ideological significance of discourse has been re-defined in terms of subjectivity, discourse itself must be considered in relation to that.

3
Discourse as subjectivity

I'm in words, made of words, others' words

Samuel Beckett,
The Unnameable

Conventional literary criticism, because it assumes poetry is to be read as the expression of an author, sees poetry as above all a matter of subjectivity, as though the question 'what is poetry?' was still nearly the same as 'What is a poet?'. But on Derrida's showing, discourse is 'a sort of machine', and subjectivity in poetry – 'the Poet' – can never be more than an *effect* of discourse, a god or ghost produced (by the reading) from the machine. The idea of the 'works of a poet' should provide no difficulties here. It corresponds to a real object, a grouping of texts that have stylistic homogeneity (as well as heterogeneity). A problem arises only when criticism tries to make an 'individual' poet the origin or cause of this stylistic unity. One stumbling block this conception immediately runs into is the 'laundry list' problem: which of the writings count as works and which, such as the author's laundry lists, are denied that status? Conventional criticism resolves the problem in a circular fashion: writings which can be read plausibly for the author's presence count as works, the others don't. Another embarrassment follows from the convention of treating the author as a single, unified individual. The assumption means that stylistic heterogeneity cannot be countenanced. It has to be made over into a unity at all costs, even if there are a number of different 'selves' at work in the poetry assigned to one author, even if there are perhaps as Pound suggests 'complete masks of the self in each poem' (1960, p. 85). Via such concepts as ambiguity and irony, conventional criticism aims to reduce the heterogeneity of texts into a version of the author's (complex) self. Thus it tries to solve a problem it shouldn't have set itself in the first place. For as Barthes explains in an essay on 'The Death of the Author', in literature 'it is language which speaks, not the author' (1977, p. 143). Subjectivity must be approached not as the point of origin but as the effect of a poetic discourse.

The subject in discourse

Discourse is determined linguistically and at the same time ideologically. But it is also determined subjectively. Subjectivity is integral to all discourse and there cannot be discourse apart from subjectivity. For example: a phonologist can describe the phonemes (and so the signifiers) of a language without speaking the language in which they are structured; but even to know they *are* signifiers assumes they are a form of discourse:

> suppose that in the desert you find a stone covered with hieroglyphics. You do not doubt for a moment that, behind them, there was a subject who wrote them. But it is an error to believe that each signifier is addressed to you – this is proved by the fact you cannot understand any of it. On the other hand you define them as signifiers, by the fact that you are sure that each of these signifiers is related to each of the others. (Lacan 1977b, p. 199)

Even to grasp these signifiers *as signifiers* (hieroglyphics, not just marks made by erosion) the phonologist must construe them as a form of discourse, see them as addressed *to* someone, grasp them in terms of human intention. The signifiers are *there*, these and not others on the stone, but in themselves they are silent. Once again, the signifier in its materiality comes first, and it is only on this basis that completed meaning is possible, with signifier linked to signified to make a sign. Hence Lacan's distinction:

> For the definition of a signifier is that it represents a subject not for another subject but for another signifier. This is the

> only definition possible of the signifier as different from the sign. The sign is something that represents something for somebody, but the signifier is something that represents a subject for another signifier. (1972, p. 194)

This sounds extraordinary and paradoxical. Yet it gives the reason why communication is a 'secondary', dependent and special effect of discourse. It is only the completed sign, when signifier is lined up with signified, 'that represents something for somebody'; it is only when discourse appears transparent that an addresser can communicate a message to an addressee. But how does the signifier represent a subject for another *signifier* rather than another subject? The example of the writing on the stone helps to explain this. Here you recognize the signifier as a signifier 'addressed to you' only because each is related to each of the others. A single mark on the stone might well be an indentation made by wind. It is only when it is seen as part of a system that it becomes a signifier for a subject, addressed to someone. From this example the general conclusion is that human beings can only become subjects by entering a system of signifiers which relate to each other independently of the subject. So there is no discourse without subjectivity and no subjectivity without discourse. On this basis the Lacanian conception seeks to show how subjectivity is always constituted in relation to discourse, how the split in the subject between conscious and unconscious is brought about in and through discourse.

Evidence for the existence of the unconscious is what it always was in the psychoanalytic tradition: hypnosis, dreams, psychopathology, everyday life as it occurs in parapraxes ('Freudian slips') and jokes. Freud's attempt to theorize the unconscious, as Lacan has often pointed out, shows the unconscious working in language much more than is generally realized. As a preparation for the more difficult terrain of Lacan it will be useful to look first at an example of Freud's concern with language and the unconscious, an example that has direct implications for understanding poetry: the theory of jokes.

A joke makes possible a pleasurable release from inhibition or repression when '*a preconscious thought is given over for a moment to unconscious revision and the outcome of this is at once grasped by conscious perception*' (Freud 1976, p. 223). As explained in the section 'The Mechanism of Pleasure and the Psychogenesis of Jokes' (pp. 165–90), the specific mechanism which enables this release in the joke to work is linguistic (hence its significance for theories of discourse and the unconscious). For Freud 'the infantile is the source of the unconscious' and the joke mechanism is a form of essentially infantile play by means of which thought 'plunges into the unconscious' (p. 227) and comes back up with a joke. Noting that children are in the habit of 'treating words as things' (that is as sounds) and that the technique in many jokes consists of focusing upon 'the *sound* of the word instead of its *meaning*', Freud says we all really want to play with words and that 'when we make serious use of words we are obliged to hold ourselves back with a certain effort from this comfortable procedure' (ibid., pp. 167–8). Jokes, then, let adults be childish without censure: they 'allow the old play with words and thoughts to withstand the scrutiny of criticism'. According to this childish/adult criterion four levels of joke can be distinguished: pleasure in nonsense, jest, non-tendentious joke, tendentious joke (ibid., p. 188).

Rephrased in Saussurean terms the theory runs like this. There is an intense and original pleasure available in the activity of the signifier and thus in treating words as phonetic rather than semantic entities. Such 'pleasure in nonsense' is childish (or childlike) ('Eeny meeny miny mo . . .') but it is not confined to children. Here is part of a 'Little Richard' song:

Tooty fruity – oh rooty
Tooty fruity – oh rooty
Tooty fruity – oh rooty
Alopbopaloobop Alambamboom!

(Readers are invited to test this for pleasure by saying it to themselves.) The same pleasure in phonetic repetition of the signifier can be found if the play with sounds is cast into some form of meaning, however rudimentary. This gives rise to the jest, especially the kind in which one signifier governs two signifieds (the pun):

Question: When is a door not a door?
Answer: When it's a jar (= ajar)

In the jest 'the meaning of the sentence . . . need not be valuable or new or even good' (p. 179), and the innocent or 'non-tendentious' joke differs from the jest only in that the play of words is contained in a sentence that makes coherent sense, for example, 'We must hang together or else we will hang separately' (cf. Freud's example, in German, ibid., p. 181). Finally, there is the 'tendentious' joke, the joke with a purpose or point because the play with words releases meanings which would otherwise be inhibited or repressed.

In describing word-play as childish, Freud's account shares the ideological assumptions of an epoch. Shakespeare's plays are vigorous evidence that Elizabethan adults did not have the same degree of inhibition about 'treating words as things'. Prejudice apart, two conclusions can be drawn from the account for the purposes of this study. First, verbal repetition foregrounds the phonetic properties of language and so the materiality of the signifier. This leads to the pleasure of the joke but the same factor also is integral to poetry:

> It is also generally acknowledged that rhymes, alliterations, refrains, and other forms of repeating similar verbal sounds which occur in verse, make use of the same source of pleasure – the rediscovery of something familiar. (Freud ibid., p. 170)

Second, Freud's account supposes a polarity in discourse. At one pole (identified with the infantile, the unconscious and pleasure) signifier is linked to signifier in a pleasurable repetition of sound; at the other (that of the adult, the conscious and control) signifier is lined up with signified in completed and meaningful sentences. An account of conscious and unconscious as effects of discourse is already anticipated here. It is developed in Lacan's project of marrying Saussurean linguistics and Freudian psychoanalysis.

Syntagmatic and paradigmatic axes

In the Saussurean account of language the signified is not determined by an extra-discursive referent, nor is the signifier determined by the signified. Signifier and signified are held in relation by the 'social fact' of language. But there is still the question as to how the subject enters language, how the signifier is 'internalized' with the subject becoming able and *unable* to line it up with the signified. As far as the social fact of discourse is concerned the bond of signifier and signified ceases to be arbitrary; but it never ceases to be arbitrary for the subject. Everyday life illustrates this well in the form of parapraxes. These happen all the time, though people conspire to ignore them (it's instructive to listen to what we actually say, or try to say). In 1979 Jeremy Thorpe was tried for attempting to murder a Mr Scott, who had claimed to have had a homosexual relationship with him. On television a news reporter said in reporting the trial that 'Mr Thorpe then sugg/duceded to Mr Scott . . .', his new word running together 'suggested' and 'seduced'. The example is precisely comparable with that Freud records as *begleit–digen*, the new word said by a young man to a lady when he wanted to 'accompany' (*begleiten*) her but was afraid his offer would 'insult' (*beleidigen*) her (see 1973, p. 206). The Royal Wedding of July 1981 produced a slip witnessed by a quarter of the world's population. In trying to repeat the priest's words 'Charles Philip Arthur George . . .' the bride said 'Philip Charles Arthur George'. Psychoanalysis would claim that this betrays an unconscious preference for the father (Philip) over the son (Charles). Similar slips can happen at the typewriter. In Michael Westlake's novel *The Utopian* there is a character who consistently types 'pricniple' in place of 'principle'.

These are more striking instances of what for Lacan is a constant process, 'an incessant sliding of the signified under the signifier' (1977a, p. 154). An example is the way a given signifier designates different signifieds in different contexts, as the sound-image 'horse' does when it is lined up with varying signifieds in: 'horse play', 'horse chestnut', 'horse power', 'horse sense', 'a Trojan horse', 'a stalking horse', 'a wooden horse', 'a clothes horse', the dead 'horse' not to be flogged and the gift 'horse' not to be looked in the mouth, the 'horse' whip feared by unwilling bridegrooms, the 'horse' of 'I gotta horse' and of *The Horse Soldiers* and *A Man Called Horse*, the 'horse' illegally sold in white packets. And such sliding does not yet include the homophone 'hoarse' for the husky voice, nor the minute phonemic substitution producing 'hoars', a poetic usage for what winter frost does to trees, as well as 'whores', on which Shakespeare frequently puns (horse/whores).

If the signified is always capable of sliding under the signifier, the question is how they line up together for the subject to be able to speak and write coherently. In Saussure's account the relationship of signifier and signified becomes stabilized as signifiers are strung together sequentially along a temporal line. Language has two axes, the syntagmatic or 'horizontal' axis and the paradigmatic or 'vertical' axis. On these two axes the syntagmatic chain of 'I met Ike' with some paradigmatic substitutions dependent on the term 'met' can be diagrammed as follows:

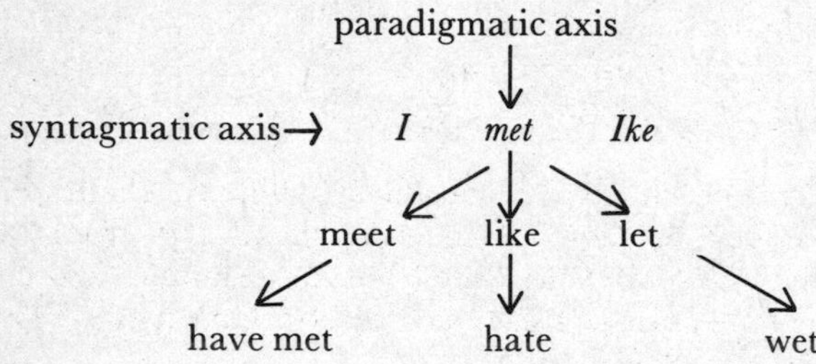

Different meanings are brought about along the syntagmatic chain – the differences between 'I met Ike', 'I like Ike', 'I wet Ike'. However, syntagmatic and paradigmatic axes are mutually dependent: any term in the syntagmatic chain can only be there in place of another from the paradigmatic or vertical axis which could be substituted for it. Saussure identified the syntagmatic chain with discourse itself while noting that each word in discourse 'will unconsciously (French: *inconsciemment*) call to mind a host of other words' which occur down the vertical axis in an 'inner storehouse' of 'associative relations' (1959, p. 123). Saussure puts these firmly aside as being 'outside discourse', that is, outside *coherent* discourse. (Saussure in fact refers throughout to the paradigmatic axis as the *associative* axis, though paradigmatic has become the conventional term in modern linguistics). This syntagmatic/paradigmatic distinction and the ensuing opposition between what is coherent discourse and what is not become the grounds on which Lacan asserts that the development of subjectivity can only take place in relation to discourse and so the split into conscious and unconscious is an effect of discourse. For Lacan the coherence of the subject – its place as intending meaning – is produced along the syntagmatic chain. Here the subject is developed as 'a single voice' sustaining meaning and itself sustained in 'this linearity'; for 'it is in the chain of the signifier that the meaning "insists"' in and for the subject (1977a, pp. 153–4). But the coherence of the subject at any given moment depends upon and is inseparable from the 'rest' of language (what Saussure categorized as being 'outside discourse').

This dependence occurs in at least the following respects:

- a signifier (e.g. a phoneme) is *there*, present for the subject in the syntagmatic chain only as a result of the absence of others against which it is differentially defined (because, in other words, in order to say /big/ we positively *don't* say /pig/, /dig/ or /gig/ etc.);
- meaning can be intended along the syntagmatic chain only because associated signifiers offering themselves from the paradigmatic axis are held aside (thus, for example, in order to say /met/ we positively *don't* say /meet/, /have met/, /like/, /hate/, /let/, /wet/, etc., etc.);
- since from each unit, each point, in the syntagmatic chain there is 'a whole articulation of relevant contexts suspended "vertically"' (Lacan 1977a, p. 154), since, that is, any signifier which takes its place in a given syntagmatic chain, a given context, carries with it its associations from other contexts (see the example of 'horse' above), these also have to be excluded from the chain for this signifier to be lined up with a signified to produce a specific meaning;
- the meaning continued from moment to moment along the syntagmatic chain depends upon the systematicity of language itself (for example, syntactic rules) of which it is the product.

All of these absences and dependencies which have to be barred in order for meaning to take place constitute what Lacan designates as the *Other*. The presence of meaning along the syntagmatic chain necessarily depends upon the absence of the Other, the rest of language, from the syntagmatic chain. And so, to complete the quotation partly used earlier:

> we can say that it is in the chain of the signifier that the meaning 'insists' but that none of its elements 'consists' in the signification of which it is at the moment capable. (ibid., p. 153)

By 'chain of the signifier' Lacan means the syntagmatic axis, 'the linearity that Saussure holds to be constitutive of the chain of discourse' (ibid., p. 154).

It is important to note that the syntagmatic chain is not to be identified with the sentence. Sentences pertain to the syntactic rules of a language, according to which they are formed correctly or incorrectly. The syntagmatic chain does operate within the sentence but it also operates beyond the sentence in the way sentences become cohesive as discourse. For example 'I hate pigs' is a sentence correctly generated within the rules of English syntax. Extension of the syntagmatic chain with another sentence (such as either 'However, I like horses' or 'Last week I got busted') would firmly identify the chain as belonging to agricultural or to bohemian discourse.

Once again here the point can be made that communication is one specific and partial effect of discourse but cannot be equated with its activity as a whole. Conscious intention is brought about along the syntagmatic chain where meaning 'insists' but this place is always produced as an effect of the Other, which remains outside it and so to that extent unconscious. The concept is not easy to grasp nor easy to express. One metaphor for it might be this: the island is only there because the sea is withdrawn. Another might be: for Lacan the ego – constituted in the syntagmatic chain – can never step over its own feet. In Freud the ego is developed through a split (*Spaltung*) in the subject between conscious and unconscious. Lacan redefines this split as a bar between the syntagmatic chain and the Other on whose grounds the chain takes place, all the other possible meanings, which are the condition of *this* meaning.

The Lacanian unconscious is not the Other itself but is rather a function of it and is included in it as its discourse: '*the unconscious is the discourse of the Other*' (1977b, p. 131; 1977a, p. 55). Such discourse is particularly manifest in substitutions of one signifier for another down the paradigmatic axis and maintains Saussure's principle that a word 'will unconsciously call to mind a host of other words' down the vertical axis. So the television reporter at the Thorpe trial was lined up for 'suggested' along the chain when a slip down the paradigmatic axis found the associated signifier 'seduced' and it came out in the newly coined signifier 'sugg/duceded'. Lacan defines 'the unconscious' as 'a play of the signifier' (1977b, p. 130) and as 'the sum of the effects of speech on a subject, at the level at which the subject constitutes himself (*sic*) out of the effects of the signifier' (ibid., p. 126).

There is a strong tradition which considers the ego to be transcendent. In contrast, the Lacanian conception insists that subjectivity and discourse are integral to each other. Accordingly, the ego cannot be transcendent, for it is brought about as a position in discourse. To exemplify this Lacan has referred to what he names as *the mirror stage*, a phase between six and eighteen months during which the human infant will greet its image in a mirror with intense excitement. The version of identity and the ego suggested by this example can be opposed to a more traditional philosophic view. In the following passage Wittgenstein takes up the question of subject and object, of me and the world:

> If I write a book called *The World as I found it*, I should have to include a report on my body, and should have to say which parts were subordinate to my will, and which were not, etc., this being a method of isolating the subject, or rather of showing that in an important sense there is no subject; for it alone could *not* be mentioned in that book . . . this is exactly like the case of the eye and the visual field. But really you do *not* see the eye. (1961, p. 117)

Wittgenstein says you do not see the eye because you see with it; all you can see in a mirror is a reflection of your eye. The eye which looks *at* the mirror is not the eye of the image *in* the mirror. Wittgenstein treats this as evidence that the ego is transcendental ('a metaphysical subject'); Lacan does not. Instead he defines identity as a *process*, one strung out between subject and object. The subject's ego is 'that which is reflected of his (*sic*) form in his objects' (Lacan 1977a, p. 194). Thus in the example of the mirror stage I am neither the eye which sees, nor the reflection seen; rather I am the very process or movement between the two, an identity produced in a structure of alienation.

This conception has two related consequences. One is that I look in a mirror and recognize what I see there as myself ('it's me!') rather than as a reflection optically produced. This is the state of the Imaginary and can be compared with that of Narcissus, who fell in love with his own image in a pool. A second implication is this. However it may appear in the Imaginary, identity is never simply itself ('it's me') but is always only a likeness, a reflection of something else. So I never recognize myself but only *misrecognize* myself. Yet even though the image in the mirror is not me, still I must identify myself in this since it is only there and nowhere else that I can be present to myself at all. Misrecognition is necessary since I can have no other identity. And without identity I cannot speak.

Althusser's account of ideology can now be better explained. In ideology subjects are produced so as to 'see' themselves as the origins of action. This effect is the result of misrecognition, of the Imaginary state in which I see the image produced optically in the mirror as me.

Enunciation and enounced

The mirror stage exemplifies the Lacanian conception of subjectivity and the structuring of the ego in relation to vision. As such it has been successfully exploited for understanding the cinema (see Metz 1975). But the analysis of poetry requires an account of subjectivity specifically in relation to linguistic discourse. It is therefore appropriate to consider relevant work in linguistics, especially that of Benveniste.

The question of subjectivity in language is most obviously posed by the use of pronouns. While Indo-European languages generally inherit a grammatical notion that there are three persons, first, second and third, Benveniste points out that Arabic grammarians consider the first person ('the one who speaks') as coupled to the second ('the one who is addressed') and contrasted with the third ('the one who is absent'). Accordingly he argues that

> very generally, person is inherent only in the positions 'I' and 'you'. The third person, by virtue of its very structure, is the

> non-personal form of verbal inflection. . . . They contrast as members of a correlation, the *correlation of personality*: 'I-you' possesses the sign of person; 'he' lacks it. (1971, pp. 199–200).

Benveniste defines *enunciation* as the act of utterance in which there takes place 'the individual conversion of language into discourse' (1974, p. 81); and he refers to these 'signs of person' as 'the formal apparatus of enunciation'. Subsequently Todorov (1981) has expanded the list of signs of person to include: first and second person pronouns (I/you); demonstratives (this/that); 'relative' adverbs (here/there) and adjectives; the present tense; 'performative' verbs (e.g. 'I swear that . . .'); modalizing terms ('perhaps', 'certainly'). These are *marks* of enunciation, those features of discourse which exhibit 'the imprint of the process of enunciation in the utterance' (ibid., p. 324). On the basis of the opposition between the grammatical presence or absence of 'the sign of person' Benveniste contrasts two modes of enunciation, *discours* and *histoire*:

> We shall define historical narration as the mode of utterance that excludes every 'autobiographical' linguistic form. The historian will never say *je* or *tu* or *maintenant*, because he will never make use of the formal apparatus of discourse (*discours*), which resides primarily in the relationship of the persons *je:tu*. Hence we shall find only the forms of the 'third person' in a historical narrative (*histoire*) strictly followed. (1971, pp. 206–7)

Discours is defined as:

> every utterance (*énonciation*) assuming a speaker and a hearer, and in the speaker, the intention of influencing the other in some way. (pp. 208–9)

In the case of *histoire* there necessarily continues to be enunciation but the speaker is in effect absent, the facts are presented as they are supposed to occur and 'the narrator does not intervene' (p. 209). Citing a passage from Balzac, Benveniste asserts: 'no one speaks here; the events seem to narrate themselves' (p. 208).

As has been pointed out both by Geoffrey Nowell-Smith (1976) and by Colin MacCabe (1981) this account of subjectivity and language is unsatisfactory because it rests on a false distinction between 'objective' and 'subjective' discourse, between one mode (*histoire*) in which subjectivity is absent, and another (*discours*) in which it is present. But *all discourse presupposes the subject* since a signifier is 'that which represents the subject for another signifier'. The 'impersonal' mode of objective description typified in the writing of history provides a position for the subject in the supposed transparency of its discourse, even though it does not contain 'signs of person', i.e. marks of enunciation. Equally, the 'personal' mode offers a subject position that cannot be reduced into an equation with the marks of enunciation it bears. The distinction between *histoire* and *discours* (the terms must stay in French) is valuable for the analysis of discourse. But it is only a distinction as to whether *marks* of person are present or absent in a discourse and does not give at all an adequate account of subjectivity and discourse.

The 'signs of person' and marks of enunciation discussed by Benveniste and Todorov are also known as *deictics* or *shifters*, linguistic forms that exhibit 'the spatio-temporal perspective of the speaker' (Traugott and Pratt 1980, p. 275). In an essay on shifters in 1957 Roman Jakobson discriminates between 'the speech act (procés de l'énonciation)' and 'the narrated event (procés de l'énoncé)':

> four terms are to be distinguished: a narrated event (E^n), a speech event (E^s), a participant of the narrated event (P^n), and a participant of the speech event (P^s), whether addresser or addressee. (1971b, pp. 133–4)

Anglicizing rather than translating the French terms we can distinguish: the *enounced* (*énoncé*, the narrated event); the *enunciation* (*énonciation*, the speech event); *subject of the enounced* (the participant of the narrated event); *subject of the enunciation* (the participant of the speech event, the speaking subject, the producer of meaning). So if I say or write 'She was there yesterday', the 'narrated event' or the *enounced* is the meaning or statement 'She was there yesterday' and 'She' is the *subject of the enounced.* The 'speech event', the act of uttering these words in language is the *enunciation*, and the person who says 'She was there yesterday' is the *subject of the enunciation.* As I sit here typing 'She was there yesterday', I am placed as subject of the enunciation. But you, gentle reader, wherever you are in my absence, when you read this 'She was there yesterday', *you* take the position of subject of the enunciation because you produce the meaning. Whether as speaker/hearer/reader/writer, for every discourse, for every poem, there must be a speaking subject who occupies the place of subject of enunciation in what Benveniste calls 'the unceasing present of enunciation' (1974, p. 84).

As signified is to signifier, so enounced is to enunciation. The enounced is what is uttered, stated or narrated, while enunciation is the act of utterance in discourse (what Jakobson calls 'the speech act'). The terms enunciation/enounced are preferable to, say, enunciation/statement because they stress that the two planes or orders are defined against each other. Just as signified depends on the signifier, so enounced depends on enunciation. But while the term signifier implies a static unit, enunciation specifies discourse as a material process. It is a *process* because discourse is sustained along the syntagmatic chain in time, and it is a *material* process because the condition for this temporal development is the material relationship of the signifiers to each other.

Jakobson's distinction between enunciation and enounced has been developed in a number of directions. However, in naming the two positions of subject of enounced and subject of enunciation it says nothing about the relation of subjectivity and discourse, about the way subjects are installed into the two different positions. It is left for Lacan to ask, 'Is the place that I occupy as the subject of a signifier concentric or ex-centric, in relation to the place I occupy as subject of the signified?' (1977a, p. 165). The answer he gives for discourse corresponds exactly to his account of identity and vision as exemplified in the mirror stage. Thus: I identify myself in discourse; this is never a full identity but always partial, a misrecognition; yet it is the only identity I can ever have. Along the syntagmatic chain the ego finds a coherent position for itself as 'subject of the signified' (or enounced); but this position is subordinate to the place it occupies as subject of the signifier. Signified depends on signifier, enounced upon the process of enunciation. The subject of the enounced is therefore a smaller circle contained inside ('concentric' to) the subject of the enunciation, a larger circle, which lies outside it (is 'ex-centric' to it). 'Subject *of*' may be better understood as 'subject *for*'. *Subject of the enounced and subject of enunciation are two different positions for a speaking subject which is split between them in discourse.* The reason we can't consistently use 'subject for' is that it suggests that there is a subject outside or prior to discourse which only subsequently and secondarily becomes a subject for discourse.

As exemplum of the way that the subject of or for the enounced and the subject of or for enunciation are always necessarily different and disjunct positions, Lacan refers to the supposed paradox in which someone admits they are lying:

> a too formal logical thinking introduces absurdities, even an antinomy of reason in the statement *I am lying*, whereas everyone knows that there is no such thing.
>
> It is quite wrong to reply to this *I am lying* – If you say, *I am lying*, you are telling the truth, and therefore you are not lying, and so on. It is quite clear that the *I am lying*, despite its paradox, is perfectly valid. Indeed, the *I* of the enunciation is not the same as the *I* of the statement (*énoncé*), that is to say, the shifter which, in the statement, designates him.
>
> (1977b, p. 139)

Thus, for example, a man under interrogation who has been lying may break down and admit 'I am lying'. He means that the liar is, as it were, someone else represented in his discourse, though the single shifter of the first person covers both I's. The situation would be even clearer if he said 'I have been lying', discarding one self and adopting another, that is, speaking about his previous untruthful self as a character in his own discourse as much as to say 'he was lying, not me'. The 'I' speaking and the 'I' spoken about can never be the same.

Identity is ever only possible as misrecognition. For vision, I can only see myself in a mirror by seeing this reflection from somewhere else. For discourse, I can only identify myself in discourse by speaking about this character ('myself') from somewhere else; the 'I' as represented in discourse (subject of the enounced) is always sliding away from the 'I' doing the speaking (subject of enunciation). The latter precedes or is 'ex-centric' to the former.

So, for the subject of the enounced: the word is treated as

meaning; signifier is lined up with signified; the syntagmatic chain is carefully sustained in its linearity; discourse appears transparent; subjectivity becomes *centred*, finding a fixed position where the ego is apparently present to itself. For the subject of enunciation: the word is treated as thing; the signified slides under the signifier; the syntagmatic chain is fissured and broken; discourse is revealed as a material process; subjectivity becomes *decentred*, as the fixed position of the ego is shown to be a temporary point in the process of the Other. In the Lacanian conception these two positions or 'states' are designated as the *Imaginary* and the *Symbolic*. Like Blake's Innocence and Experience they are contraries defined in relation to each other. In Colin MacCabe's summary: 'As speaking subjects we constantly oscillate between the symbolic and the imaginary – constantly imagining ourselves granting some full meaning to the words we speak, and constantly being surprised to find them determined by relations outside our control' (1976, p. 14). The Imaginary and the Symbolic, repetition of identity and difference, are terms of a dialectic, both necessary for the construction of human subjectivity.

On the basis of the preceding we can reconsider the *histoire/discours* distinction. Lacan's example of 'I am lying' is definitely *discours* but the analysis applies equally to *histoire*. The impersonal mode of he/she/it or the personal mode of I/you can both provide a coherent position for the subject of the enounced if the discourse aims to deny enunciation and give transparent access to the enounced. *Discours/histoire* is a lesser and dependent distinction, and should be understood as a distinction *within* the enounced. This is evidenced by the ease with which one mode can be rewritten as the other with only minor alterations. Michèle Barrett and Jean Radford re-write part of a Dorothy Richardson novel to show that '"she" and "her" . . . can be transposed into the personal mode "I/my" without further alterations to the passage' (1979, I, p. 268). And in his 'Structural Analysis of Narratives' Barthes demonstrates that 'the whole of the beginning of *Goldfinger*, though written in the third person, is in fact "spoken" by James Bond' (1977, p. 112). Of the extracts from poetry examined in this present work two – the ballad and a passage from Pope – begin as *histoire* but slip over into *discours* in the last lines.

The enounced of a discourse always contains a narrator, an implicit 'speaker', as Todorov explains:

> The narrator is . . . he or she who places certain descriptions before others, although these preceded them in the chronology of the story. It is he or she who makes us see the action through the eyes of this or that character, or indeed through his or her own eyes. . . . (cited Belsey 1980, p. 30)

In *histoire*, the impersonal mode, the narrator is implicit; in *discours*, the personal mode, the narrator is presented explicitly. In *histoire* there is a narrator and what is narrated, with the narrated given priority; in *discours* there is a *represented speaker* and what he or she talks about, with the speaker given priority. This second, first person *discours*, is a crucial instance for poetry since it includes those cases in which the reader is invited into simple identification with a represented speaker.

A position as subject of the enounced is always disjunct from that as subject of enunciation. This conception of how subjectivity is structured in discourse means three things when applied to the study of a poetic discourse.

1 A discourse can seek to deny this disjunction entirely and to offer a position to the reader exclusively as a transcendental ego. The English bourgeois poetic tradition is just such a discourse. It can be defined precisely as a regime of representation aiming to disavow enunciation so as to promote only a position as subject of the enounced, especially when it creates the effect of an individual voice 'really' speaking by concealing the way it is produced as an effect. This invites misrecognition, one that conventional literary criticism colludes in whenever it pronounces of a poem that 'Shakespeare says here . . .' or 'Wordsworth is now speaking about . . .'. Such a reading treats the poem as a manifestation of 'presence' even when it really knows it's only a poem. It is a perverse reading in the strict sense, and works through a fetishistic structure Barthes has formulated as '"I know these are only words, but all the same . . ."' (1976, p. 47).

2 Enunciation is a material process, its time an 'unceasing present' in Benveniste's phrase. A reader therefore is always

positioned in enunciation as its subject, and this means that he or she always in fact produces the poem in a present reading, just as actors and technicians produce a play from a script. But the act of producing can be disavowed and responsibility for the poem attributed to 'The Poet'. In so far as the reader ascribes the origin of a poem to what can never be more than a position represented in it, misrecognizing the text as what 'Shakespeare says' etc., to that extent the reader becomes alienated from his or her own productive energies.

3 The disjunction of enunciation and enounced has one other consequence. Although, as the second part of this book will argue in detail, English poetic discourse is constructed to offer an absolute position to the reader as transcendental ego, there is no guarantee that the effect will be produced. All the various circumlocutions – 'offering a position', 'aiming to provide', 'seeking to' – are needed because a discourse can never fully impose itself and is always exceeded in the reading. Any fixed position in the enounced is always sliding away from enunciation in the present. So however much a poem claims to be the property of a speaker represented in it, the poem finally belongs to the reader producing it in a reading. The whole enterprise of Part Two is to read the poetic discourse *against* the way it presents itself to be read.

Discourse, then, is cohesive and determined simultaneously in three respects: materially, ideologically, subjectively. English poetic discourse is materially determined, having a certain consistent shaping of the signifier inscribed in it. By the same token it is ideologically determined, being a product of history, a relatively autonomous tradition, a bourgeois form of discourse. It is also subjectively determined and is a product of the reader, for whom it offers a position as transcendental ego. This it works for both positively and negatively: positively, by aiming for closure in the syntagmatic chain and promoting a coherent position as the subject of the enounced; negatively, by seeking through historically varied strategies to hold back the process of enunciation. There is a consistent relation between enounced and enunciation throughout the discourse. And this relation in turn is founded in a version of line organization specific to the discourse, iambic pentameter.

Part II
English poetry

4
Iambic pentameter

> to break the pentameter, that was
> the first heave
>
> Pound,
> *Canto 81*

The Russian Formalists and the Prague School of linguists considered the one universal condition of poetry, its constitutive principle or *dominanta*, to be its organization into lines. Tomashevsky writes:

> Contemporary European practice retains the habit of printing verse in arbitrary and equal lines, and even sets them off with capital letters; by contrast prose is printed in unbroken lines. Despite the dichotomy between writing and speech this fact is significant since in speech certain associations are bound up with the written form. This breaking up of poetic language into lines, into sound units of similar and possibly equal force, is clearly the distinctive feature of poetic language. (1965, p. 155)

In poetry the line boundary is not arbitrary but is determined by a system of equivalences operating from line to line. In different languages and cultures line equivalence or metre is established on different bases. Four main systems can be distinguished: the number of syllables in a line, syllable duration, tone, stress. So in Hungarian folk poetry the only requirement for an utterance to constitute a line is that it should have six syllables. Classical Greek and Latin poetry is organized with recurring patterns of long and short syllables. Chinese is a predominantly monosyllabic language with a very limited number of syllables but it quadruples its syllabic resources because each may occur in four different tones (level, rising, rising and falling, level and falling). Classical Chinese poetry is organized mainly with four-, five- and seven-syllable lines patterned through an opposition between the level tone and the other three 'deflected' tones in a binary opposition of even and non-even. In Old, Middle and Modern English poetry the main organizing principle is stress, though this is not as uncomplicated a feature as native speakers usually assume.

Systems rarely operate through only one principle of organization. One may be dominant, but is often mixed with others. In Modern English, iambic pentameter requires both a patterning of stressed and unstressed syllables and a set number of syllables per line. And while the classical metres of Greek and Latin are predominantly made up through syllable duration some influence of stress is present, though this remains a matter of controversy: 'the very idea of the presence of stress accent as an ingredient in the construction of Latin verse is not more than a hypothesis accepted fairly consistently by German and English classicists, but denied with equal consistency by their French and Italian colleagues' (Cole 1972, p. 86).

Besides these four main principles others are possible. Classical Hebrew poetry, for example, is made up with end-stopped lines divided by a caesura into two parts or *cola*. These are related in a complex system of synonymous and antithetic parallelism which is semantic and syntactic. In this it remains an exception to the general rule by which in different languages the poetic line is organized *phonetically*, that is, in terms of the physical properties of language. Thus metre generally inscribes precedence of the signifier into the very basis of poetry. As Lacan comments in referring to a stanza by Valéry:

> This modern verse is ordered according to the same law of the parallelism of the signifier that creates the harmony governing the primitive Slavic epic or the most refined Chinese poetry. (1977a, p. 155)

If the material basis of poetry is recognized in metre, in the 'parallelism of the signifier', the ensuing question must be how different metres are historically specific.

In 1912 Ezra Pound set himself the principle of composing 'in the sequence of the musical phrase, not in sequence of a metronome' (1963, p. 3). A generation later Brecht, in an essay of 1939, rejected 'the oily smoothness of the usual five-foot iambic metre' (iambic pentameter in German and English are closely comparable) and describes how he 'gave up iambics entirely and applied firm but irregular rhythms' (1964, p. 116). The political contrast of fascist and communist, Pound and Brecht, is so striking it obscures the grounds they share. Both reject liberalism and the notion of the transcendental ego. For Brecht 'the continuity of the ego is a myth' (ibid., p. 15), while according to Pound, 'One says "I am" this, that, or the other, and with the words scarcely uttered one ceases to be that thing' (1960, p. 85). Both champion oriental art forms as a means to criticize and oppose the Western Renaissance tradition, the bourgeois tradition. Both advocate free verse.

Their work provides a point from which to interrogate the traditional prosody of English poetry, accentual-syllabic metre, most typically represented by iambic pentameter. Despite significant historical developments in practice – notably Augustan correctness in the couplet followed by Romantic relaxation – there is a solid institutional continuity of the pentameter in England from the Renaissance to at least 1900. Like linear perspective in graphic art and Western harmony in music, the pentameter may be an epochal form, one co-terminous with bourgeois culture from the Renaissance till now.

Yet the free verse practice of Pound and Eliot opens a gap at the margin of the traditional prosody which is usually closed as follows: pentameter is normal in Modern English because it arises naturally from the English language itself. Prised away from its home in poetry, pentameter becomes immediately re-naturalized in language. This view, widely diffused and casually repeated, mainly derives from what even now remains the standard work, Saintsbury's *History of English Prosody* in three volumes, 1906–1910. Saintsbury's premise is that 'every language has the prosody which it deserves' (vol. 1, p. 371) and so iambic metre corresponds to the inherent rhythms of the English language. Established first by Chaucer, it was obscured during the fourteenth and fifteenth centuries due to linguistic change, particularly the 'lopping off of the final syllable' (ibid., p. 292); but with this uncertainty resolved, iambic metre (like the British Constitution in the Whig theory of history) emerged naturally in what Saintsbury calls 'an unbroken process of development' (ibid., p. 372).

One may argue against this linguistic determinism in two ways. First, even if it is true that a language gets the prosody it deserves, *another* metre may claim to be more natural to English. Besides iambic pentameter there is the older accentual four-stress metre inherited from Old English poetry. While the pentameter, conventionally defined as a line of ten syllables alternately unstressed and stressed, legislates for both stress and syllable, accentual metre requires only that the line should contain four stressed syllables and says nothing about the unstressed syllables. Since stress or syllable prominence is phonetically much more significant in English than syllable duration, accentual metre has a strong claim to be more natural in Old, Middle and Modern English. Its case is vigorously put by Northrop Frye, among others:

> A four-stress line seems to be inherent in the structure of the English language. It is the prevailing rhythm of the earlier poetry, though it changes its scheme from alliteration to rhyme in Middle English; it is the common rhythm of popular poetry in all periods, of ballads and of most nursery rhymes. (1957, p. 251)

Second, iambic pentameter did not simply emerge from the language: it was an historical invention. In fact it was invented twice. The first time was in the fourteenth century when it took the form of Chaucer's Middle English pentameter. Between then and the early sixteenth century massive phonological changes took place in the development of Modern English from Middle English, so that poets could no longer discern Chaucer's metre and the pentameter was re-introduced. Wyatt and Surrey translated Italian sonnets by Petrarch into English and into iambic pentameter; Surrey later used the metre in the form of blank verse to translate some of the *Aeneid*. Both poets are published in *Tottel's Miscellany* of 1557, by which date the hegemony of the new metre is so complete that Wyatt's metrical errors – if that's what they are – appear in corrected form. Accentual metre, the old four-stress line, was pushed aside by the ascendency of the pentameter and other accentual-syllabic metres at the Renaissance, as Saintsbury well knew, since he says that its establishment the second time was due to 'Italian influence, classical influence, and the two as combined and reflected by Spenser' (1910, I, p. 303). Promoted into dominance by the new courtly culture, pentameter is an historically constituted institution. It is not natural to English poetry but is a specific cultural phenomenon, a discursive form.

In rejecting Saintsbury's assumption that language determines metre there is no need to deny all determining force exercised by language on metre. Modern English clearly constitutes a precondition for pentameter, as can be seen in several ways. Stress is an important linguistic feature in Modern English and pentameter exploits it. Stress is inherent in the isolated word when it is of more than one syllable, and a full account of this is offered by Halle and Keyser (1971). They give the rules we operate in knowing how to place primary stress by saying 'América' instead of 'Améríca', 'arthrítis' not 'árthritis', and so on. As soon as isolated words are combined into phrases the stress they hold in isolation is modified by context. A form of this is isochrony: the tendency to keep roughly the same time-interval between stresses so that (in Attridge's excellent illustration 1982) the two syllables of *Jóhn stánds* is timed roughly the same as the six of *Jónathan understánds*, both having two strong stresses, in contrast to *Jóhnny Bláck withstánds*, which has three. There is also a preference for alternating strong and weak stresses to give 'bright and shining eyes' rather than 'shining and bright eyes' with two strong stresses adjacent (see Bolinger 1965). In prescribing a regular spacing-out of stress along the line pentameter makes use of the tendency to isochrony and preference for alternation in Modern English. So of course does its ancient rival, the four-stress line. In fact this accentual metre exploits English more obviously and readily than pentameter. Not concerned with unstressed syllables, it accommodates itself easily to the way isochrony demotes syllables between stresses, while pentameter insists on them, being concerned with the number of syllables in a line. Modern English, then, is *a* determinant for iambic pentameter but not the only determinant.

Pentameter and language

Since Saintsbury, and particularly since a symposium in the *Kenyon Review* in 1956, linguists have contributed to the analysis of metre as well as literary critics. A section of *Style in Language* (see Jakobson 1960) dealt with metre and the concern has been continued in three anthologies: Chatman and Levin (1967), Freeman (1970), and Chatman (1971). Books which form part of the discussion include Epstein and Hawkes (1959), Chatman (1965), Halle and Keyser (1971) and Fowler (1966 and 1971). A very recent addition is the scrupulous and constructive book by Attridge (1982). Somewhat against this consensus, work by Crystal (1969 and 1975) has sustained the insistence of the Russian Formalists and later Mukařovský (1933) on the crucial importance of intonation in defining poetic line and metre.

This project (which is far from unified) of analysing metre has suffered from taking English pentameter as its almost exclusive object, only rarely making comparative reference to other metres (classical, English accentual, free verse). It has also been impaired by its theoretical presuppositions, particularly a willingness to conceive metre atomistically in terms of the metrical units making up the line rather than holistically (in the tradition of the Formalists) as an effect of the line itself. In attacking this dominant approach David Crystal has been provoked to challenge: 'On what grounds, other than tradition, has stress been singled out from the other phonological features of verse and been identified with metre?' (1975, p. 110). It is hard sometimes to resist the view that Latin hexameter – even with references to 'feet' – operates as a clandestine model for English metre. Although definite progress has been made in giving an accurate linguistic description of iambic pentameter, the dominant mode of approach by linguistics has had two consequences, both of which can be criticized. I shall pursue each criticism some way since they concern the two central factors for the definition of pentameter, intonation and abstract pattern.

1 In the linguistic discussion iambic pentameter has been seen as essentially a matter of syllable and stress. Trager and Smith (1951) advanced a concept of stress as a relative variation in four degrees of loudness, independent from pitch and juncture, and this work became central to the metrical discussion. Not

only was stress given priority as the predominant feature of metre but sometimes it was treated effectively as though it were fixed, as in the model of Latin syllable duration, rather than conforming to the 'principle of relativity' as Jespersen affirmed originally in 1900 (Chatman and Levin 1967, p. 77). Stress is certainly not simply a matter of amplitude – loudness – for if it were, strictly understood, an 'unstressed' syllable would be silent. In any case stress is not the only or even perhaps the main means in English by which a syllable is emphasized and so made available for use in the pentameter pattern. There is also intonation or 'tone of voice'. As Delattre points out with a vivid example (Bolinger 1972, p. 160), intonation marks the spoken difference between a polite inquiry about the evening menu

What shall we have for dinner, mother?

and a recommendation of cannibalism

What shall we have for dinner . . . mother?

A syllable can be emphasized by means of stress but also by *accent*, that is, through its place in one of the many strongly varied intonation contours of English. The relation of stress and accent remains controversial in linguistics. David Crystal argues that both stress and accent are produced by a 'bundle' of phonetic features, not just one, and that in 'stress, the dominant perceptual component is loudness' while in accent it is pitch (1969, p. 120). *Both stress and accent* have to be considered together in defining what makes a syllable more or less prominent in an utterance. Roger Fowler (1971, p. 175) summarizes four factors contributing to syllable prominence: that inherent in the isolated word when it is of more than one syllable (cf. Halle and Keyser 1971); that due to a sub-sentence stereotyping, for instance of the kind which prefers 'bright and shining eyes' to 'shining and bright eyes'; that ensuing when a word is picked out for emphasis for semantic reasons (as intonation signals difference of meaning in Delattre's example); that which occurs through the normal functioning of intonation contour.

The difficult topic of intonation will have to be explored but it is more appropriately left for discussion of Pound and free verse or 'intonational metre' as I shall prefer to call it (see chapter 9 below). Enough has been said here about stress and accent to draw two conclusions. First, the concept of stress alone is entirely insufficient to explain syllable prominence, and accent as effected holistically by the intonation contour must be considered as well. Second, if only because of the role of intonation, syllables do not occur in a simple contrast between prominent and unprominent but have degrees of prominence relativized by the context. Prominence and unprominence do not function like bricks added together to make a wall but like the relative values attaching to pieces in a game of chess, all such values being changed when one is lost (or added). With this qualification, I shall avoid the awkward terms prominence/unprominence and continue to use the term *stress* to mean syllable prominence, however achieved; and I shall refer to intonation to point to the relative degrees of stress (i.e. prominence) in an utterance as it would occur outside a metrical context, if it were just spoken in conversation.

2 Another doubtful development in linguistic work on metre also follows from giving theoretical priority to syllable and stress, to units within the line rather than the line itself. One area of the discussion has come to operate on the basis of an epistemological error. This is the 'generative metrics' of Halle and Keyser (1966 and 1971), Magnuson and Ryder (1970 and 1971), Kiparsky and – ironically – Attridge (1982) (ironically because in his second chapter on 'Linguistic Approaches' Attridge provides one of the best critiques of the procedure). The theoretical principle of this tendency is explicit when Halle and Keyser announce:

> We propose below a set of principles or rules which by their nature yield a large variety of metrical patterns, in the same way that rules of syntax yield a large variety of syntactic patterns. (Freeman 1970, p. 371)

The assumption is that each line of pentameter actualizes the rules of metre in the same way that rules in transformational grammar can show how sentences are generated through transformations in the relations between surface and deep structures. The hoped for result is 'acceptable' and 'unacceptable' lines of pentameter on the model of grammatical and ungrammatical sentences. But pentameter is not a structure elaborated by rules into specific examples: it is a *gestalt* or pattern perceived, a 'set' of expectations confirmed or denied generally. Unlike the rules of transformational grammar, the metrical pattern of pentameter is culturally explicit and institutionalized, and has been since at least 1575 when George Gascoigne in *Certayne Notes of Instruction concerning the making of verse or rhyme in English* made the confident remark:

> Note you that commonly now a dayes we use none other but a foote of two sillables, whereof the first is depressed or made short, & the second is elevate or made long: and that sound or scanning continueth throughout the verse. (cited Thompson 1961, p. 71).

On this principle, that of the perception of a *gestalt*, any line in a passage of iambic pentameter tends to become iambic pentameter. Raymond Chapman points out the way a sentence from daily speech ('the stated price is subject to review') can turn into pentameter when inserted into that metrical context:

> At last he rose and twitched his mantle blue:
> Thĕ státĕd príce is̆ súbjĕct tó rĕviéw.
>
> (1973, p. 94)

But the same utterance – the same intonation – will also function perfectly as a four-stress line in accentual metre:

> Little maid, pretty maid, whither goest thou?
> Down in the meadow to milk my cow.
> Shall I go with thee? No, not you,
> The státed príce is súbject to revíew.

In both cases the set of metric expectations imposes itself on the same utterance to make an acceptable line in two different metres. The metre makes the line while the line supports the metre.

That definitions of pentameter should begin with the culturally established pattern is shown by the fact that the pentameter norm can be perceived entirely apart from lines – that is, in prose. Commenting in detail on a passage from Virginia Woolf's novel *Mrs Dalloway* Traugott and Pratt note that

> phrase 8 ('and plunged at Bourton into the open air') has an

> equally regular alternation of single unstressed and stressed syllables, that is, iambic feet. No one familiar with English verse can miss the iambic rhythm in phrase 8, or the fact that the phrase is a line of perfect iambic pentameter, with routine elision of unstressed *the* with stressed *ópĕn*. (1980, p. 79)

An even more impressive instance occurs in a speech by Vladimir in *Waiting for Godot* beginning 'Let us not waste our time in idle discourse'. This establishes the 'idea' of the pentameter in association with a certain humanist rhetoric only in order tó mock both. A number of regular 'lines' ('. . . thŏse críes fŏr hélp stĭll ríngĭng ín ŏur eárs!') lead via parody of the most famous line of pentameter in English ('What are we doing here, *that* is the question') to a deliberate breaking of the pattern with the iambically impossible anapaestic 'line', 'We are waiting for Godot to come –'.

The normative dominance of pentameter will persist in a passage of verse until it is deposed by another norm established against it, such as Pound's free verse, which insists on breaking with pentameter; or is so dissipated by enjambement, trochaic endings, hypermetry, etc., that it finally vanishes into prose. This happens less often than people think, as would have been apparent if the linguistic discussion of metre had paid more attention to free verse. As Graham Hough has shown (1960) much of what passes for free verse, including Eliot's 'Prufrock' and one of Lawrence's more polemically free verse poems, turn out on examination to be in loose iambic pentameter. As he says, 'the attractive force of the iambic decasyllable is so great that the rhythm slips into it' (p. 97), which is why Pound speaks of the heave needed to break the pentameter.

These two general criticisms of work on metre concern intonation and the pattern of pentameter. The implications lead back to a definition of pentameter as counterpoint. As applied to pentameter the term *metre* has meant ambiguously the 'official' metrical pattern itself (ten syllables alternately unstressed and stressed) and the pattern as *practised* in relation to syllables made prominent in the intonation of a line. Both in fact are needed to specify the pentameter, which is defined by *the relation of two systems*, the abstract metrical pattern and the intonation of non-metrical language. On this there is a definite consensus among linguists and literary critics. In 1949 Wellek and Warren wrote that:

> English verse is largely determined by the counterpoint between the imposed phrasing, the rhythmical impulse, and the actual speech rhythm conditioned by phrasal divisions. (1963, p. 170)

More recently, introducing a selection of articles on metre, Chatman and Levin summarize a now general agreement:

> The further inference, again recognized in almost every article, is that one has to do with *two* systems in any performance of a poem, the metrical system (with its events and prominences), and the suprasegmental system of English (with its stresses, intonations and junctures, however they are analyzed). These co-existent systems are given different names: meter *vs* performance, (traditional) meter *vs* 'rhythm' (potential or core), meter *vs* its actualization, abstract frame *vs* actual instance, schema or 'normative fact' *vs* particular, etc. Similarly the relationship between them is named variously: tension, interplay, counterpoint. But despite the variation in terminology, the principle is the same, and the solidarity of view inspires confidence in the validity of the distinction. (1967, pp. 69–70)

The term *counterpoint* is preferred here because of the currency given it first by Hopkins and later by Yvor Winters. It designates the metre as function of two forces, the vector between two axes. One is the abstract pattern

ti-tum ti-tum ti-tum ti-tum ti-tum,

a grid of expectations explicitly formulated within British culture and sufficiently confirmed within a poem to fix the pattern as totalized *gestalt*. The grid enables both

How sweet the moonlight sleeps upon this bank!

and

O monstrous act! Villany, villany, villany!

to constitute pentameter, even though, as E. M. W. Tillyard says in citing them, the lines are 'as different as they can be except in that the pattern behind them is the same' (1929, p. 18). On the other side there are the prominences and unprominences of the syllables produced in the non-metric usage. It is not the case that the official pattern is a metrical 'abstraction' and its practice in counterpoint an 'actualization' of this abstraction; rather the counterpoint *is* the metre.

This can be substantiated through two comparisons.

1 English pentameter can be compared with the model of classical hexameter. The abstract pattern of Latin hexameter is defined by the *Oxford Classical Dictionary* as follows:

> Its first four feet may be dactyls or spondees, its fifth is regularly a dactyl, its sixth a spondee or a trochee. (1970, p. 684)

Lines are measured in numbers of syllables with duration as the basis of contrast in a binary opposition between long and short, long being equal to two short. Thus:

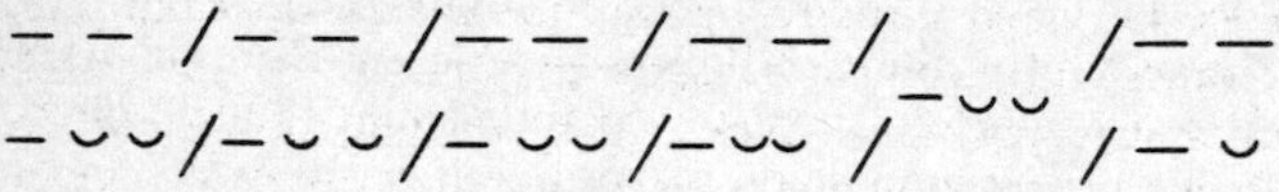

— — / — — / — — / — — /   / — —
                                      — ⏑ ⏑
— ⏑ ⏑ / — ⏑ ⏑ / — ⏑ ⏑ / — ⏑ ⏑ /   / — ⏑

After following rules for elision this becomes:

— —|—   ⏑ ⏑| — ‖ — | — ⏑ ⏑| — ⏑ ⏑| — ⏑
tendebantque manus‖ rip(ae) ulterioris amore.
(*Aeneid* VI. 314)

And that one might almost say is that. *The abstract pattern is always actualized*, except in the case of Catullus and those who *refuse* to put a dactyl at the fifth foot ('an Alexandrian mannerism', as the *Oxford Classical Dictionary* notes). The term *metre* accurately includes both the abstraction and its actualization, and the composition of Latin verse becomes a mechanical operation in which slots in the abstract pattern are filled using a Latin dictionary, which defines the correct length of each syllable, and *Gradus Ad Parnassum*, a special dictionary for verse composition, which gives metrical synonyms. Contrast with this model shows how the English pentameter works.

In English, the abstract pattern is ten syllables, alternately unstressed and stressed. In the Latin model, length of syllable is absolute and durational contrast is binary (not least because

Latin makes use of the contrast syntactically and semantically). But as the earlier discussion of accent and intonation sought to show, syllables in English do not occur in a simple binary contrast between prominence and unprominence, and degrees of prominence in an utterance are always contextually relative. Since syllable prominence is relative, it follows that the abstract pattern of pentameter is *never* actualized (except of course by the line boundary) but that syllable prominences and unprominences in the non-metric intonation approximate it. This approximation *is* the metre.

2 Pentameter can be compared with the older, accentual metre, a comparison which confirms that pentameter is to be defined by approximation rather than coincidence between abstract pattern and non-metrical intonation. The abstract pattern of four-stress accentual metre anticipates four equally prominent syllables in each line. Since numbers of unstressed syllables are not regarded as significant for metrical purposes, syllable prominence provided already by the non-metric intonation of an utterance will readily and *necessarily* coincide with some of these four metric positions. Where they do not, or do not do so sufficiently strongly, the expectations set up by the abstract pattern will intensify what stress there is, as it did to the sentence, 'The stated price is subject to review' when this was inserted into the context of accentual metre. As a result, prominences anticipated by the abstract pattern and those pre-existing from non-metric intonation will *coincide and reinforce* each other. Hence the high prominence of syllable, the heavily stressed rhythms, of accentual verse:

> / / / ◡ ◡ /
> Sing, sing what shall I sing?
> ◡ / ◡ ◡ / ◡ ◡ / ◡ ◡ /
> The cat's run away with the pudding-bag string.

Here a line of six syllables and one of eleven constitute two metrically regular lines in a metre specified by reinforcement, not counterpoint.

Pentameter *can* be performed as though it were accentual metre; that is, thumped out as doggerel so that abstract pattern and intonation coincide. This is how children and the inexperienced, used mainly to accentual metre (for example, nursery rhymes), generally speak pentameter. But this is not pentameter. A poetry in which intonation and abstract pattern sufficiently coincided for the two to reinforce each other as in accentual metre would, as Wimsatt remarks, provide the basis for a metre *other* than pentameter: 'the "norm" of iambic pentameter could, by being persistently actualized, become the "rule" of a different metre' (Chatman 1971, p. 211). To repeat: pentameter is specified by counterpoint.

Spoken performance of pentameter is accordingly open to variation in a way accentual verse is not. Since pentameter consists neither of the abstract pattern itself nor the intonation of non-metric language but is a function of the two in which both are active, actual performance will vary widely according to whether the voice tends towards the abstract pattern (though never losing hold on the intonation) or towards the intonation (though it could only become non-metric speech by defying entirely the abstract pattern).

Pentameter and ideology

The preceding review of current linguistic and other analyses of pentameter has aimed to define the metre and show how it is determined linguistically. As a discursive form pentameter is also determined ideologically. In *Mythologies* Barthes argues that an important ideological operation of a discourse is the way it seeks to 'naturalize' itself as 'myth' by disclaiming its ideological operation. Pentameter is precisely such an example of 'myth' for it seeks to nestle all but invisibly in an equivalence with poetry itself, as Barthes has tried to suggest – somewhat confusedly – is the case with the French alexandrine (1972, p. 133 footnote). Pentameter is widely read merely as a signifier denoting the signified 'this discourse is poetry', its avowed function being no more than the need to determine line boundaries. But this sign ('pentameter means poetry') elides (and would conceal) *two* equations: (a) poetry consists of lines (the material nature of poetry); (b) pentameter is one historically determined form of line organization (and there are others). The metre can be seen not as a neutral form of poetic necessity but a specific historical form producing certain meanings and acting to exclude others.

These meanings are ideological. Though they persist in and with the metre, they surface most manifestly during its founding moment, at the Renaissance. Pentameter comes to power as a neo-classical form and this is inscribed into its defining feature of counterpoint. On the one side, as the name proclaims, iambic pentameter reaches back to the quantitative metre of Greek and Latin and the model of binarily contrasted syllables arranged in 'feet'; on the other, the non-metric intonation approximates to the abstract pattern and thus the native language is brought into relation with the classical model. So a particular practice of the national tongue can dress itself in the clothes of antiquity and a bourgeois national aspiration may represent itself in the form of universal civilization (see Kristeva 1974, p. 210). The pentameter is favoured by the English court at the Renaissance – in 1589 Puttenham praises Wyatt and Surrey on the grounds that

> they greatly pollished our rude & homely maner of vulgar Poesie, from that it had bene before, and for that cause may iustly be sayd the first reformers of our English metre and stile. (1968, pp. 48–9)

The ascendency of pentameter relegates the older accentual metre to a subordinate or oppositional position in which it has remained ever since: the appropriate metre for nursery rhymes, the lore of schoolchildren, ballad, industrial folk song and even, more recently, the football chant:

City, City, what's the score?
City! ( ) what's the score?

Once established as national poetic institution pentameter becomes a hegemonic form. It becomes a sign which includes and excludes, sanctions and denigrates, for it discriminates the 'properly' poetic from the 'improperly' poetic, Poetry from verse. In an unbroken continuity from the Renaissance to 1900 and beyond, a poem within the metrical tradition identifies itself (in Puttenham's words) with polish and reformed manners as against poetry in another metre which can be characterized as rude, homely, and in the modern sense, vulgar.

The hegemony of pentameter continues to promote certain meanings rather than others:

1 *Abstraction* Relative to accentual metre whose requirement of four stresses admits a wide variety of line lengths, the abstract pattern of pentameter is abstract in a specific and restricted fashion. It represents a systemic totality, an explicit preconception legislating for every unit of stress and syllable, and this 'continueth throughout the verse' (Gascoigne), 'in sequence of a metronome' (Pound). The only relief from this uniformity is the intonation, which even so always implies the comprehensive grid to which it approximates. Pentameter accordingly shares the prestige attaching to abstract and uniform modes. Marshall McLuhan has suggested an historical significance for such modes; the heterogeneity and simultaneity of feudal culture, its 'easy habit of configuration',

> yields with the Renaissance to continuous, lineal and uniform sequences for time and space and personal relationships alike. (1962, p. 14)

Iambic pentameter takes its place within this development and corresponds to other innovations in representation and ideology. Linear perspective, as McLuhan says, presupposes an explicit and abstractable system which precedes any actual representation, a uniformity from which no detail of the two-dimensional surface can escape. Similarly, everything spoken of in pentameter must be spoken 'through' the relatively rigid abstract pattern of the metre. The epistemological implications of this have been traced out by Pound. In rejecting pentameter as metronomic he affirms absolute rhythm, 'a rhythm, that is, in poetry which corresponds exactly to the emotion or shade of emotion to be expressed' (Pound 1963, p. 9); poetry must give everything its 'precise rendering' in a rhythmic equivalent and every convention must be trampled if it impedes such rendering. With a different positive perspective Brecht also attacks the imposed uniformity of iambic metre and protests against the ensuing 'smoothness and harmony of conventional poetry' which inhibits the showing of 'human dealings as contradictory' (1964, p. 116). Both poets attribute a universalizing, essentializing tendency to pentameter.

2 *Concealed production* Yet the abstraction of pentameter is never openly announced as such. According to the contradictory nature of the metre, counterpoint being its specific effect, the abstraction of the pattern is always produced in relation to the apparent spontaneity of the intonation contours in ordinary speech. To this extent the severity of the abstract pattern is always mitigated. The 'smoothness' Brecht notes, the tendency of verse in iambic metre to 'glide past the ear' because its (regular) rhythms 'fail . . . to cut deep enough' (1964, p. 120), has been welcomed as desirable for the English poetic tradition. As early as 1557 one of Tottel's 'Uncertain Authors' praises Petrarch for his 'lively gift of flowing eloquence'; as late as 1938 Louis MacNeice defends 'regular kinds of verse' on the grounds that 'if you are going to poise your phrases at all they will usually need more poise than can be given them by the mere arranging of them in lines' (1938, p. 117). Unruffled smoothness, flowing eloquence, poise: these are qualities the counterpoint of pentameter facilitates in two respects. Through counterpoint the abstract pattern of the metre is relatively backgrounded. Recognition of the work of metric *production* – and so of the poem as constructed artifice – is suppressed in favour of a notion of the poem as spontaneously generated *product*. Pentameter can be seen as a mechanism by which the poem aims to deny its production as a poem, a mechanism therefore that promotes commodity fetishism. At the same time a cultural meaning becomes attached to the poem's speaker/reader. Counterpoint requires that a complex abstract pattern be performed as though it were extemporary. The pattern learned by effort is presented as though it were unstudied, the contrivance is made to seem habitual, the speaker's impersonal and superior tone appears effortless.

3 *Necessity and freedom* Pentameter carries what might be called a constitutionalist significance. Saintsbury says that in the counterpoint of pentameter 'the claims of Order and Liberty are jointly met as in no other metrical form is ever possible (1910, vol. 1, p. 345), a significance that has been noticed since, as for example when Halle and Keyser write that

> the iambic pattern allows for a great deal of freedom while at the same time providing sufficient constraints to make the art

> form an interesting one for the poet to work in. (1971, p. 171)

Robert Graves and Laura Riding have made an explicit claim for the political significance of counterpoint:

> Metre considered as a set pattern approved by convention will stand for the claims of society as at present organized: the variations on metre will stand for the claims of the individual. (1925, p. 24)

In pentameter intonation approximates to the abstract pattern but can never coincide with it. Because of this feature, as the previous quotations show, counterpoint has yet another ideological connotation. For it corresponds to the ideological opposition between the 'social' and the 'individual', an opposition which envisages society as a 'necessity' against and within which the individual finds his or her 'freedom'.

4 *Proper speaking* Pentameter makes verse especially compatible with the 'Received Pronunciation' of Standard English (the bourgeois norm). It does so because it legislates for the number of syllables in the line and therefore cancels elision, making transition at word junctures difficult. E. L. Epstein explains the effect with reference to a well known line from Pope's 'Essay on Criticism', 'When *Ajax* strives, some Rocks' vast Weight to throw' (l. 370). In three places ('Ajax-strives', 'strives-some', 'weight-to') similar sounds end one word and begin the next:

> Normally (that is, in casual discourse), there would be no problem; the first of the similar sounds would be omitted by a variety of elision . . . it might sound something like, 'When Ajak'strive' some Rock's vast Weigh'to throw'. (1978, p. 44)

However, the 'formal style of poetry reading, even in silent reading' means that this elision does not operate and so to say 'Ajax-strives' without elision 'requires a pause, an actual "cessation of phonation"' (ibid., p. 44). This is an extreme example of a feature typical of English poetic discourse. Elision of some degree is invited whenever the sound at the end of one word and that at the beginning of the next is close in point of articulation. For example in the first line of Shakespeare's 'Sonnet 73', 'That time of year thou may'st in me behold', a casual or vernacular elision is invited at several points: 'tha'time', 'ti-mov', 'thoum-ayst', 'stin-me', 'meeb'hold'. This is prohibited by Received Pronunciation. Epstein attributes the cancellation of elision in formal style to 'a reader's socially inherited competence in the reading of poetry'. Such competence is motivated linguistically by pentameter because it requires full pronunciation to be given to every syllable, thus discouraging elision and demanding cessation of phonation between similar sounds at word boundaries. This all sounds sufficiently abstract and is only a way to describe what the ear tells us already – that the canon asks for a clipped, precise and fastidious elocution. Such pronunciation – one thinks of Laurence Olivier – signals 'proper' speech; that is, a class dialect. Pentameter aims to preclude shouting and 'improper' excitement; it enhances the poise of a moderate yet uplifted tone of voice, an individual voice self-possessed, self-controlled, impersonally self-expressive. The topic of pronunciation takes analysis of ideological meanings right up to the question of subjectivity and subject position.

Pentameter and subjectivity

As was argued in chapter 3, a discourse may work to provide a subject position for the reader as transcendental ego. Such a position is made available when the syntagmatic axis of the discourse is constructed in a careful and unified linearity. Meaning 'insists' along the syntagmatic axis, and so the attempt to close meaning along this axis offers a coherent position to the subject as 'a single voice' sustaining meaning and itself sustained in 'this linearity' (Lacan 1977a, pp. 153–4). The fixity of this position for the ego appears transcendental – simply *there* rather than constructed – when the process of discourse which in fact produces the position is generally backgrounded and denied.

Relative to other metres, English iambic pentameter is a syntagmatic form and works to promote a position for the reader as transcendental ego. It does so while operating in the material basis of poetry, its specific and constitutive principle, the line. In expanding these assertions it will be useful to bear in mind a contrast between pentameter and the older four-stress metre, as well as the model of classical metre.

The way pentameter enforces coherence and unity in meaning has been convincingly evidenced by Donald Davie. Taking Pound's free verse exploration of a landscape, 'Provincia Deserta', Davie re-writes it in iambic pentameter (1965, pp. 60–3). The whole exercise needs to be read but some salient points can be picked out: 'the pentameter makes the creeping and peering happen together, whereas in Pound's poem the man is seen first to creep, and then to peer. . . . In the blank verse we are told that the Dronne has lilies in it; we do not discover it for ourselves as the speaker did. In Pound's poem the speaker sees the road wind eastwards, and then reflects that Aubeterre is where it leads to. . . . In the blank verse Aubeterre and the road are parts of a single act . . .'. Davie's conclusion is that:

> Pound's lineation points up the distinctness of each image or action as it occurs, and thus insists on the sequence they occur in, whereas blank verse, by speeding up the sequence, blurs them together. (p. 62)

The effect of pentameter is to run together and unify (Davie's word is 'interweave') subject matter and meaning.

The reason for this is that while all metre is precisely linear, an organization along the line closing at the line boundary, pentameter is linear to a special degree. It points horizontally along the syntagmatic chain. This is the case both within the line and across lines. Within the line Paul Kiparsky has pointed to the relative nature of stress in pentameter,

> the fact that the degree of stress is not absolute but exists by virtue of the greater or lesser stresses next to it – 'syntagmatically' – (rather than by virtue of the greater or lesser stresses that might have occured instead of it – 'paradigmatically'). . . . (1977, p. 194)

In the Latin verse model preformed units of long and short syllables can be substituted in the line without otherwise affecting the metre. This cannot happen with pentameter (as anyone knows who's tried it) because pentameter depends upon syllable prominence and this is relative to context – the preformed units are modified by their position and reciprocally modify the rest of the line. The syntagmatic tendency persists across lines, as Attridge explains. While the four-stress line tends to break down into two-beat units as well as building cohesively into two- and four-line units, the pentameter line resists both dismantling into smaller units (since if it does divide, the units are unequal, one of two and one of three stresses) and cohesive assemblage into larger units. Each pentameter line tends to retain its separate identity:

> This means that when we reach the end of the line there is no compelling pressure from the larger structure to register the completion of a rhythmic unit and to move on to the next one. Instead, the syntax has a more powerful voice . . . and will determine whether we pause or read straight on to the following line. (1982, p. 133)

Pentameter allows the syntax 'a more powerful voice'; compared to other metres it is a *syntagmatic form*. And since coherence in the subject is an effect of meaning intended along the syntagmatic chain, iambic pentameter in verse will support and promote coherence in the subject.

The predominantly syntagmatic structuring of pentameter determines subject position in two ways simultaneously. These can be distinguished according to whether counterpoint is thought 'up' from the intonation towards the abstract pattern or 'down' from the pattern onto the intonation. On one side that abstract pattern will always make available a consistent and autonomous position 'above' the local commitments and intensities enacted in the stresses of the intonation. Through counterpoint these intensities are brought into relation with the externalized linearity of the abstract pattern and are lifted into a kind of transcendence. Evidence for this is Yeats's well known discussion of how traditional metres (typified by the pentameter) render the personal as impersonal:

> Pound, Turner, Lawrence wrote admirable free verse, I could not. I would lose myself . . . all that is personal soon rots; it must be packed in ice or salt. . . . If I wrote of personal love or sorrow in free verse, or in any rhythm that left it unchanged, amid all its accidence, I would be full of self-contempt because of my egotism. . . . (1961, p. 522)

The single voice that 'comes most naturally when we soliloquize' tends to be over-personal; through 'a powerful and passionate syntax' enforced by traditional metres the voice can be raised towards 'impersonal meditation'. That is: syntagmatic closure promoted by the pentameter can approximate to a poise and self-consistency that seems absolute (Yeats identifies it with art, the ideal, impersonality and indeed eternity). But on the other side this autonomy is effected by the pentameter only at the cost of increased repression: the abstract pattern contains and overrides process as enacted in the intonation. In fact Wordsworth and Coleridge, whose programmatic commitments might have been expected to lead them to free verse, both make finely conservative spokesmen for the repressive effectivity of what their practice reveals to be essentially traditional pentameter. Coleridge traces the origin of metre to that 'spontaneous effort' of the mind 'which strives to hold in check the workings of passion' (1949, II, p. 49); Wordsworth takes the view that excitement may get out of control ('be carried beyond its proper bounds') and that metre has 'great efficacy in tempering and restraining the passion' (1965, p. 264).

Pentameter fosters this control because contrasted with other metres it would even out intonation along the line. It lowers peaks of stress and raises troughs: lowers, because even the nuclear tone of the intonation must submit to the even repetition of the abstract pattern; raises, because in the slower pace of the pentameter line intermediate stresses become more felt. G. N. Leech cites Kipling's line 'And the dawn comes up like thunder outa China crosst the bay' and shows it can be read either as a four-stress line (∪∪´∪∪∪´∪∪∪´∪∪∪´) or iambic octameter (´∪̣´∪̣´∪̣´∪̣´∪̣´∪̣´∪̣´). He explains:

> If the speed is slowed down, however, intermediate stresses make themselves felt . . . , causing the listener to reinterpret the passage in two-syllable measures. This should cause no wonder, since it is a well-known fact of English rhythm that the slower the speed at which an utterance is spoken, the greater the proportion of stressed to unstressed syllables. (1969, p. 117)

But pentameter requires this slower pace since its abstract pattern looks for a binary uniformity of stressed and unstressed syllables. It acts to restrain, to withold and release stress in an even distribution through the line ('an even distribution through the line). The intonation of an extra-metric utterance ('Tye up the knocker, say I'm sick, I'm dead') rising to two equal peaks ('I'm sick, I'm dead') is ironed out by the abstract pattern of the metre. Accordingly pentameter provides space for certain polysyllabic words and so encourages a certain vocabulary and register in poetry. (A full account of this would be the subject of another study along lines laid down by Mukařovský, 1964, pp. 113–32).

To sum up: accentual metre preceded pentameter in English and became subordinated to it at the Renaissance though continuing in popular forms such as children's rhymes:

> Eaver Weaver, chimney sweeper,
> Had a wife and couldn't keep her,
> Had another, didn't love her,
> Up the chimney he did shove her.
> (Opie 1967, p. 20)

In accentual metre the stress of the intonation and the abstract pattern coincide and reinforce each other; in pentameter they are counterpointed. The coincidence in accentual metre calls for an emphatic, heavily stressed performance, one typically recited or chanted, often in association with rhythmic gestures, clapping, dancing. In chanting, rhythmic repetitions take complete priority over natural intonation, subsuming it, and this is the metrical 'space' for a collective voice (see Attridge 1982, p. 88): since a group of speakers reading a poem tend to speak together in 'choral reading' (see Boomsliter 1973), a poem that offers itself for chanting ('Eaver Weaver, chimney sweeper') provides for collective speaking. There is only one way to speak the line and the metre denies space to the individual voice except to join a pre-given order it cannot modify. In significant contrast, the counterpoint of pentameter is a function of two opposed requirements, those of the abstract pattern and the non-metric intonation, between which any performance is free to find its own inflection. Instead of the collective voice of accentual metre pentameter gives space to the 'natural' intonation and so to a single voice in the closure of its own coherence. Try speaking 'Humpty-Dumpty' and then Milton on his blindness ('When I consider how my light is spent', etc.).

F. R. Leavis was right to assert that English poetry in the dominant discourse 'depends upon the play of the natural sense movement and intonation against the verse structure' (1967, p. 50); by accommodating 'idiomatic speech' (ibid.) poetry becomes as though transparent to the presence of a represented speaker, an effect 'as if words as words withdrew themselves from the focus of our attention and we were directly aware of a tissue of feelings and perceptions' (p. 47). Four-stress metre – and for that matter free verse – forces attention to the words as words and so shatters any effect of transparency.

Relative to other forms of discourse all poetry can be seen to foreground the signifier. In four-stress accentual metre (to persist with the example) the coinciding reinforcement of abstract pattern and intonation puts the sound of the words before their meaning – it exhibits metricality and openly celebrates rhythmic pleasure in the work/play of the signifier. In contrast, pentameter would disavow its own metricality and restrain the activity of the signifier. In this lies the central effect of pentameter, an effect which can be made visible by reference to the distinction between enunciation and enounced as developed in Chapter 3. There is always necessarily a disjunction for the subject between its position as subject of and for the enounced and its position as subject of and for the enunciation (on which the former position depends). When I speak a line of poetry (such as that of the Milton sonnet just now) I am placed as subject of the process of enunciation and only thus may come to occupy a place as subject of the enounced, 'Milton' considering his blindness. Iambic pentameter works to deny the position of subject of enunciation in favour of that of the subject of the enounced; *it would disclaim the voice speaking the poem in favour of the voice represented in the poem, speaking what it says*. Accordingly pentameter is able to promote representation of someone 'really' speaking. It rose to dominance at the Renaissance through its capacity to represent an individual voice in the same way that music and song changed to accommodate a new 'realism':

> The late medieval composer had not attempted to reproduce the accent and intonation of human speech when he set a text.

> The words were so many syllables, to be fitted to music which followed its own laws of construction . . . By the early sixteenth century, this attitude was rapidly changing. Both the humanists and the Reformers were closely concerned with words; and a new realism had come to dominate the fine arts. Composers, too, began to obey the prosody of natural speech in setting words to music. (Trowell 1963, II, p. 18)

By eliding metricality in favour of 'the prosody of natural speech' the pentameter would render poetic discourse transparent, aiming to identify the speaking of a poem with the speaking of a represented speaker or a narrator; it invites the reader into a position of imaginary *identification* with this single voice, this represented presence.

The discussion of pentameter has meant to show the cohesion of English bourgeois poetic discourse by analysing iambic pentameter as a necessary condition of its possibility. The dominance of the metre since the Renaissance gives it a claim to be an epochal form, and a similar analysis might be made of other metres considered 'natural' to a language but which are in fact each a product of bourgeois culture: the French alexandrine, German pentameter, hendecasyllabics in Italian and Spanish, the Russian tetrameter (for some such work on the alexandrine, see Roubaud 1978).

In leaving the question of metre two points of qualification need to be made. First, iambic pentameter, by far the most widely used form, has been taken to typify accentual-syllabic metre in English. There has been no account of other iambic forms or of the other metres, trochaic, anapaestic and dactylic. I see no reason to doubt Martin Halpern's conclusion that these all resolve themselves into two types:

> of the four so-called 'syllable-stress' metres in English – iambic, trochaic, anapaestic and dactylic – only the iambic has developed in a direction radically different from the native accentual tradition . . . the other three, as characteristically used in English poetry, are simply variants of the strong-stress mode. (1962, p. 177)

Second, there has been a degree of abstraction at work in analysing iambic pentameter apart from its use in a particular moment of the historical process. The abstraction has been necessary. It is a temporary and provisional 'freezing' of other factors in order to isolate and understand the material effect of the metrical form. Of course in practice the metre is always active in conjunction with many other features. Clearly, in the aggressive early days of the struggle for bourgeois hegemony, especially around 1600, the pentameter had a novelty and glamour that was long gone in 1900. Now the pentameter is a dead form and its continued use (e.g. by Philip Larkin) is in the strict sense reactionary. Eliot wrote in 1942: 'only a bad poet would welcome free verse as a liberation from form. It was a revolt against dead form, and a preparation for new form' (1957, p. 37).

The cohesive identity of English poetic discourse continues through historical change. To deal with this I shall look at four sample texts from four crucial conjunctures in the history of the discourse: the Renaissance, obviously enough the founding moment of the discourse and so particularly likely to show how it works; the 'high plateau' of the discourse when it was consolidated during the Augustan period; its renovation by Romanticism, when changes are introduced whose effect is to keep it the same; and finally the crisis of the discourse when the Modernist revolution challenges it at every level.

English poetic discourse is rooted in the pentameter. Through it certain ideological meanings and a subject position are 'written into' the discourse. Pentameter defends the canon against the four-stress popular metre, which foregrounds the poem as a poem; it promotes the 'realist' effect of an individual voice 'actually' speaking. To provide this, a position for the reader as subject of the enounced must be fixed in a coherence, a stability 'of its own'. Fixity is achieved mainly in two ways: as signifier is held firmly onto signified in the syntagmatic chain, as the work/play of the signifier is denied. Here are to be found the relevant terms for analysing historical variation with reference to the four examples. Each chapter will begin with a discussion of attitudes towards language in each period. Other related topics and terms for their analysis – the *referential effect* and *iconicity*, for example – will be introduced and explained as they come up.

It is not easy to shake off the familiar assumptions brought into play by the traditional canon. To set up a strong point of contrast to the dominant tradition and to show historical development before the founding of the tradition I shall begin with a medieval ballad. The two forms – ballad and the Renaissance courtly poem – exemplify opposed kinds of discourse: one collective, popular, intersubjective, accepting the text as a poem to be performed; the other individualist, elitist, privatized, offering the text as representation of a voice speaking.

5
The feudal ballad

> The least acquaintance with the subject will recall a great many commonplace verses, which each ballad-maker has unceremoniously appropriated to himself, thereby greatly facilitating his own task, and at the same time degrading his art by his slovenly use of overscotched phrases.
>
> Walter Scott,
> *Minstrelsy* (1830)
> (cited Bold 1979)

Ballad as oral poetry

The language of the medieval ballad is generally conceived at present as 'oral' rather than 'literary' or written. By referring back to Derrida's account of the relation between speech and writing I shall argue that the oral medium does not account for the nature of ballad style and that it must be grasped as a separate mode of discourse, one offering a position for the subject as relative rather than absolute and transcendental. A number of topics, such as rhyme, are introduced which will take on greater significance later when they are contrasted with practices in the bourgeois tradition.

Alan Bold provides an example of the conventional account of the ballad:

> The simple rhymes, the incremental repetitions, the obligatory epithets, the magical numbers, the nuncupative testa-

> ments (*i.e. deathbed bequeathals*), the commonplace phrases, the reliance on dialogue, the dramatic nature of the narrative: these make the ballad easier to remember, easier to memorize. The unique style of the ballads derives from its oral nature. Literary poetry, written for the page, depends on the unexpected phrase, the ingenious rhyme, the contrived figure of speech. Literary poets like to invent; oral poets depend on formulas. (1979, p. 14)

The full implications of a distinction between 'oral' and 'print' consciousness are drawn out in Walter J. Ong's *Orality and Literacy* (1982), another volume in this present series. Here I am concerned with the way the conventional account, exemplified by Bold, repeats the main assumptions of the so-called Parry–Lord theory of 'oral-formulaic' poetry.

Milman Parry, an American classical scholar, noticed the recurrence of stock phrases and epithets in Homer, the 'wine-dark sea' and 'swift-footed Achilles' for example, and guessed that this use of 'formulae' was evidence that the poems were composed orally. For confirmation he turned to the study of the heroic poetry of Yugoslav folk-song. The singer could perform thousands of lines of this verse, and there was no question of recall – the poem was being composed as it was sung. This was possible, so it was argued, because the poet was able to put together much of the poem from a restricted 'vocabulary' of formulaic phrases and motifs. Parry died before he published his research, and his work was completed by his pupil, Albert B. Lord, in *The Singer of Tales* (1960).

The 'oral formulaic' theory must be rejected for several reasons. In the first place it is a version of 'technological determinism' in assuming that discourse is essentially determined by its *medium* of expression – as Bold puts it, 'the unique style of the ballads *derives* from its oral nature' (my italics). To make this claim the Parry–Lord theory relies on a complete opposition between the categories of 'the oral' and 'the written'. The opposition cannot be maintained in the face of Derrida's demonstration that the graphematic is a feature of both writing *and* speech, including, so he says, 'the most "event-ridden" utterance there is' (1977, p. 192). As performed orally the ballad is certainly that. (At this point the reader may like to take advantage of the printed medium by re-reading the summary of Derrida's argument in chapter 1 above, pp. 13–15.) Moreover, there is empirical evidence against the oral-formulaic theory, especially that brought forward by Ruth Finnegan in her book *Oral Poetry* (1977). It will be convenient to deal which the text is read 'without any center or absolute anchor-tenets.

1 . . . songs are related to one another in varying degrees; not, however, in the relationship of variant to original, in spite of the recourse so often made to an erroneous concept of 'oral transmission'; for 'oral transmission', 'oral composition', 'oral creation' and 'oral performance' are all one and the same thing. (Lord 1960, p. 10)

Here Lord is attacking the view that there exists some original form of a ballad, made up either by an individual or collectively, and this is then transmitted orally. His argument is that the oral medium means that the relationship of original composition and variation in performance cannot apply to the ballad because every performance *is* an original composition. In saying this he supposes that, by contrast, a written text is composed once and for all by an author, who puts what he or she intends into it, and that every reading or performance is only a variation on this original. Derrida denies this view of writing. The graphematic feature of all language means that in the case of the written text *as well as* that of the oral there can be no one original intention in relation to which other readings can be considered only variations. On the contrary, there are only contexts in which the text is read 'without any center or absolute anchoring' (1977, p. 186).

2 For the oral poet the moment of composition is the performance. In the case of a literary poem there is a gap in time between the composition and reading or performance; in the case of the oral poem this gap does not exist, because composition and performance are two aspects of the same moment. . . . Singer, performer, composer, and poet are one under different aspects but *at the same time*. Singing, performing, composing are facets of the same art. (Lord 1960, p. 13)

There is empirical evidence against this. Referring to instances from Eskimo, Dinka and medieval Gaelic court poetry, Ruth Finnegan asserts that 'there are many recorded cases of oral poetry where its creation . . . is due to long deliberation *before* the performance' (1977, p. 80). But even if the theory were correct in saying there is no temporal gap between composition and performance, there is still a gap between what the singer intends while composing and what the audience reads out from the performance. The graphematic once again intervenes. The ballad, just as surely as the written poem, can be recorded. In fact if ballads had not been written down, particularly by Child, many would now be lost. For a generation performance has been tape-recorded, as for example Appalachian folk-song was by Alan Lomax. Today videotape can be used, so that gestures, expression and acting performance are all recorded. As Derrida states clearly, it is the sign in general and not just language which operates as 'a sort of machine', and so the fact that performance of the ballad can be recorded demonstrates that the graphematic is inescapable even here, in a most '"event-ridden" utterance'. The intention of the oral poet, even when composing and singing at once, cannot wholly permeate the text; what goes into the text in composition and what comes out in performance for a reader, even if composition and performance happen at the same time with the same singer, cannot be 'facets of the same art', as Lord claims. The Parry–Lord theory identifies together singing, performing and composing in a Romantic quest for some impossible full 'presence' of the poetic mind in the act of uttering itself apparently without mediation. This is not possible in written poetry. But nor is it possible in oral. The oral/written opposition which supports the Parry–Lord theory collapses. An alternative description of the ballad as a form of discourse needs to be found, and in fact this begins to emerge in a third feature in the Parry–Lord theory.

3 The poetic grammar of oral epic is and must be based on the formula. It is a grammar of parataxis and of frequently used and useful phrases. (Lord 1960, p. 63)

Traditionally, parataxis is distinguished from syntaxis: while Caesar's 'I came, I saw, I conquered' is paratactic, its equivalent in syntaxis would be something like 'After I had come and seen, then I conquered'. Lord claims that oral poetry selects prefabricated formulaic units and sets them alongside each other in paratactic combinations and that it does this because of the singer's need to extemporize. Even if it is true – as seems likely – that the oral poet is helped to keep the song going by the use of formula phrases, the oral medium does not account for the style since it is found also in written poetry. Ruth Finnegan cites evidence from Anglo-Saxon poetry to the effect that 'a heavily formulaic style is characteristic not just of the Old English "oral" epic of *Beowulf* but also of some *written* compositions in Old English' (1977, pp. 69–70) and that the formulaic style is characteristic of Old English poetry *tout court*. On the basis of numerous examples, including Xhosa and Zulu oral poetry, she concludes that the '"formulaic" literary style is equally possible in written literature' (ibid., p. 130). There is reason, then, to deny Lord's explanation while still accepting the accuracy of his description.

Lord compares the paratactic feature of the oral epic and the nature of language in general:

> The method of language is like that of oral poetry, substitution in the framework of the grammar. Without the metrical restrictions of the verse, language substitutes one subject for another in the nominative case, keeping the same verb, or keeping the same noun, it substitutes one verb for another. (1960, p. 35)

The 'substitutions' Lord speaks of here are those Saussure distinguishes as made down the 'vertical' or paradigmatic axis, while the 'framework of the grammar' in which the substitutions are made is the syntagmatic axis. Lord's description points accurately to the kind of discourse exemplified in the ballad. In it the syntagmatic chain does not aim for tight closure and rigid subordination of elements in a linear development; rather it works through juxtaposition, addition and parallel, typically, as we shall see, in binary and trinary patterns. Parataxis allows paradigmatic elements that would otherwise be excluded from the syntagmatic chain to appear alongside each other within it.

Far from being sufficiently explained as resulting from use of the oral medium, this feature helps to mark off the ballad – and indeed much other medieval poetry – as a separate discourse. As an aspect of discourse, the effect needs to be understood in relation to subjectivity and in terms of enunciation and enounced. Disruption in the syntagmatic chain means that the discourse of the ballad does not offer transparent access to the enounced, and so no fixed position is offered to the reader as subject of the enounced.

'Three Ravens'

This (Child 1965, I, no. 26A) is a suitable example of the medieval ballad because it is short, it is English, and it certainly existed as early as 1611, when it was printed in the collection *Melismata* edited by Thomas Ravenscroft.

Internal evidence suggests that the ballad should be read in terms of the social relations of feudalism. Hounds, hawks and doe are presented in a relationship of feudal dependence on the dead knight. The poem gives an idealized version of the bond between vassal and superior, retainer and lord, as the feudal class might wish to see it (the wish is explicit in the last two lines). At the same time, in a contradiction common in the medieval ballad, the point of view of the peasantry is also represented – the three ravens who would gladly attack the knight once he was safely dead. Further, elements of 'Three Ravens' imply early feudalism rather than late. As Jessie L. Weston has argued in *From Ritual to Romance*, the stories of the medieval Romances, and particularly those concerning Perceval, Gawain and Galahad, contain material from fertility religion: the purpose of the hero's quest is to heal or resurrect the Fisher King and so remove the curse which has left the land waste. The dead knight of 'Three Ravens' connotes both the dead Fisher King himself and the dead knight found in the Chapel Perilous in some versions. The birds of carrion and the sympathetic death of the pregnant doe link the death of the knight to a generalized sterility. And in northern mythology Odin has two ravens, Huginn and Muninn, though a more likely source for the ballad would be the ravens who flock to the battlefield in Old English poetry. 'Three Ravens' can be read confidently as a feudal form, though one containing more ancient material:

1 There were three rauens sat on a tree,
Downe a downe, hay down, hay downe
There were three rauens sat on a tree,
With a downe
There were three rauens sat on a tree,
They were as blacke as they might be.
With a downe derrie, derrie, derrie, downe, downe.

2 The one of them said to his mate,
'Where shall we our breakefast take?'

3 'Downe in yonder greene field,
There lies a knight slain vnder his shield.

4 'His hounds they lie downe at his feete,
So well they can their master keepe.

5 'His haukes they flie so eagerly,
There's no fowle dare him come nie.'

6 Downe there comes a fallow doe,
As great with yong as she might goe.

7 She lift vp his bloudy hed,
And kist his wounds that were so red.

8 She got him vp vpon her backe,
And carried him to earthen lake.

9 She buried him before the prime,
She was dead herselfe ere euen-song time.

10 God send euery gentleman,
Such haukes, such hounds, and such a leman.

Vocabulary and phrasing in 'Three Ravens' is colloquial, monosyllabic and everyday. The syntax is simple. The first nine stanzas form three sets of what are closely comparable sentence forms, each sentence contained in the stanzaic unit. The poem begins with three simple sentences ('There were . . .', 'one . . . said . . .', 'There lies . . .') though the second introduces direct speech. In the next two a main clause leads to a relative clause (in stanza 4 the meaning seems to be 'they lie down so that they can keep their master well') and in the third (stanza 6) an appositional noun clause acts as a comparative ('As great . . . as . . .'). The final syntactic triad is made up of three co-ordinated sentences with verbs in the simple past tense ('She lift vp . . . And kist . . .', 'She got him vp . . . And carried . . .') except that in the third (stanza 9) there is pure parataxis ('She buried . . . She was dead . . .').

In its paratactic structuring the ballad combines separate units. These units are not so much stock phrases and epithets as narrative ideas, elements of event, dialogue and motif. And these are well adapted for juxtaposition simply because they do tend to be unitary and self-contained. The ballad form usually lets events and dialogue stand by themselves without generalization and explanation. In the classic definition:

> A ballad is a folk-song that tells a story with stress on the crucial situation, tells it by letting the action unfold itself in event and speech, and tells it objectively with little comment or criticism of personal bias. (Gerould 1932, p. 11)

The narrative developed in the syntagmatic chain of 'Three Ravens' is presented abruptly and without comment apart from the ambiguous wish at the end: three hungry ravens, a dead knight, his hounds, his hawks, the doe, the burial of the knight, the death of the doe. The paratactic feature of this syntagmatic chain can be seen in three respects.

1 *Intertextuality* Every text is intertextual (i.e. it refers to other texts), but the ballad exhibits this in an extreme form as the individual ballad combines narrative units from others. The dead knight of 'Three Ravens' recalls the dead figure mourned in the 'Corpus Christi Carol' and there are also talking birds in 'The Carnal and the Crane' (Child 55). The motif in which the death of one lover is followed by that of the other ('She was dead herselfe ere euen-song time') recurs widely in the ballad, in 'Fair Margaret and Sweet William' (Child 74) and most famously in 'Barbara Allen' (Child 84). The refrain 'downe a downe' is also found elsewhere, in 'The Baffled Knight' (Child 112A). There is also a nursery rhyme, 'A Carrion crow sat on an Oak' found in a manuscript of 1627 (Opie and Opie 1951, number 87).

2 *Stanzaic units* It is a naive assumption – one made by Walter Scott – that because a discourse does not aim for strict syntagmatic closure it has no principles of organization. On the contrary, as David Buchan has shown (1972) the parataxis of

the ballad is drawn up in terms of binary, trinary and annular or 'framing' patterns constructed by narrative voice (whether simple narration or speech) and by narrative unit, both held strictly within the stanza. In the ten stanzas of 'Three Ravens' the typically abrupt opening stanza ('There were . . .') and the optative closure of the tenth ('God send . . .') frame the other eight. These in turn are balanced binarily against each other, stanzas 2–5 being mainly speech concerning the ravens, hounds and hawks, 6–9 being simple narration concerning the doe. There is a further binary division within each half since 2 and 3 express the ravens' wish to attack the knight, 4 and 5 the corresponding ability of hawks and hounds to defend him, while 6 and 7 describe the descent of the doe and her care for the knight, 8 and 9 her burial of him.

3 *Incremental repetition* While all language is inherently syntagmatic, the ballad operates through a particular form of progression consistent with its paratactic feature. Defined as such by F. B. Gummere in 1907, *incremental repetition* occurs when a formulaic phrase, stanza, or narrative unit is repeated with a significant addition that advances the narrative (Parry refers to 'adding style'). Caesar's 'veni, vidi, vici' is such an incremental repetition. In 'Three Ravens' narrative units, each separated into stanzas and groups of stanzas, are arranged triadically to make up a narrative development. The first three stanzas present the three ravens. The next three form an incremental repetition; 'His hounds' that 'lie' are paralleled to 'His haukes' that 'flie' until the narrative progresses at the third term with the fallow doe. And the next three stanzas (7–9) are made up in turn of six narrative units in a repetition which is both binary and trinary. There are the binary juxtapositions of 'lift'/'kist', 'got'/'carried', 'buried'/'dead', culminating dramatically in the unanticipated death of the doe herself. The whole narrative works with three sets of characters, ravens, hawks and hounds, the doe, each in relation to the dead knight. The potential aggression of the ravens is completely balanced by the potential protection of hounds and hawks, a situation of stasis removed by the intervention of the third figure, the doe, who safely buries the knight. The whole story is framed by the last stanza in which the three ravens of the first are answered by the three guardians, 'Such haukes, such hounds, and such a leman'.

This paratactic structuring leaves the enounced of the text remarkably open and contradictory. It is not clear whether the ravens speak stanzas 3–5 or all the rest (performance would not indicate the quotation marks closing stanza 5 in the written text) yet it is impossible for them to speak the last stanza. Crucially, what *becomes* of the ravens and their wish for breakfast as the narrative moves paratactically and without explanation from them to the knight and the doe?

Whereas (in Freud's topography) in the province of the conscious and preconscious there are mainly word-presentations (language), in that of the unconscious there are only thing-presentations (images) (see Freud 1957, XIV, p. 201). Although 'Three Ravens' is verbal, it consists of a series of vivid images without adequate rationalization, and so it invites reading as a fantasy or day-dream. Freud's *The Interpretation of Dreams* explains that the dream has a manifest content and a latent content. If the narrative of 'Three Ravens' is treated as manifest content, a latent content for the text can be suggested, however tentatively. The dead knight may stand for the symbolic dead father and the doe for the symbolic mother, in which case the animals and birds may be sons ('small animals and vermin represent small children' in dreams, Freud 1977, p. 474). If so, two attitudes to the father are represented: sorrowful obedience by the hounds and hawks, the desire to castrate by the ravens (would they peck out his eyes?). The text can be seen as a *compromise formation*, as Freud defines it:

> Thoughts which are mutually contradictory make no attempt to do away with each other, but persist side by side. They often combine to form condensations, *just as though there were no contradiction between them*, or arrive at compromises such as our conscious thoughts would never tolerate but such as are often admitted in our actions. (1977, p. 755)

'Three Ravens' expresses both a wish to submit to the father and at the same time a wish to kill him. This compromise formation, the unresolved contradiction between two unconscious wishes, is able to become latent because of the paratactic structuring of the text.

In Lacan's account, careful subordination of elements in the syntagmatic chain provides a fixed position for the ego as subject of the enounced. There is progression and coherence in the syntagmatic chain of 'Three Ravens' but no attempt to close the chain tightly, for example by explaining how the ravens did find breakfast in the end. Parataxis leaves the text open to associated ideas and unconscious possibilities as these are held in suspension down the paradigmatic axis.

Enunciation

As exemplified in 'Three Ravens', the medieval ballad constitutes a very different poetic discourse from that of the subsequent bourgeois tradition. In the enounced the syntagmatic chain develops paratactically through parallel and juxtaposition rather than through subordination. At the same time the irreducible dependence of enounced on the process of enunciation is displayed rather than concealed. For example, as David Buchan has suggested, the materiality of the signifier is acknowledged in the prominence given to the phonetic properties of language:

> The sound patterns, then, exercise a stronger hold on the oral poet's memory of a story than the minor incidents of a line . . . the singer does not possess the particular fixation with individual words that comes with literacy, but instead works through sounds and word-groups. (1972, p. 158)

The highly formal organization of the ballad through binary patterns and incremental repetition has already been considered. As well as through the effect of this patterning, the process of enunciation in the ballad is foregrounded in the metre, verse form and phonetic details.

Ballads are sung, and since music can dictate almost any values it wants to the intonation of the words of a song, strictly there can be no ballad metre. Nevertheless, it is possible to treat 'Three Ravens' as a purely linguistic phenomenon to see what metrical tradition it may derive from. So considered it clearly corresponds to four-stress accentual metre:

> There wére threé rauens sát on a treé,
> They wére as blácke as théy might bé.

> The one of them said to his mate,
> 'Where shall we our breakefast take?'

In this metre it makes little difference whether the final /e/ is pronounced or silent (in 'blacke', 'mate', etc). The number of syllables per line here varies from 6 to the 11 of the last line of the refrain, which would probably scan:

> With a downe derrie, derrie, derrie, downe, downe.

In Child's collection 111 ballads can be read as having four stresses per line, 179 as being in 'common measure', quatrains of four and three with the juncture at the missing 'beat' equivalent to an implied stress. If spoken, 'Three Ravens' would not have the degree of reinforcement between metre and intonation that leads the nursery rhyme to be chanted; yet its four-stress rhythm would foreground metre and so the operation of the poem as enunciation. Its metre in this is consistent with the rest of the poem.

In the verse form of 'Three Ravens' each stanza consists of a rhyming couplet, yet every stanza is an example of incremental repetition since the first line of the couplet is to be repeated three times interpolated with the refrain. Meaning and verse form are parallel, with meaning closed in the stanzaic unit. A similar close parallel between meaning and verse form is maintained inside the stanza, for there meaning is contained in the line and there are no run-on lines. Every line ends with a juncture between phrases, and in all but stanzas 2, 3, 5 and 10 the first line of the couplet would make complete sense on its own. Meaning, in both line and stanza, *concurs* with the verse form, this serving to emphasize the organization into lines and stanzas as part of the process of enunciation. Here there is a complete contrast with the later, bourgeois discourse, in which meaning runs on across line boundaries, across rhyme words, and even across stanzas, as the syntagmatic chain is carefully sustained.

Rhyme discovers a link between two words on the grounds of phonetic similarity, that is, at the level of the signifier. Although by nature the relation between signifier and signified is arbitrary, social convention holds them together. In different discourses rhyme comes to suggest a relation between signifier and signified which can be broadly classified as one of *accident*, *subordination* or *coincidence*. If rhyme occurs in non-poetic discourses, it is treated as an irrelevant accident, as when someone out for a walk happens to say something like 'Put the dog on the log'. Because it is an effect of the signifier and so always risks showing the precedence of the signifier, rhyme is acknowledged in prose by the care taken to avoid it, precisely to treat it as incidental.

In an essay on 'Rhyme and Reason' W. K. Wimsatt (1970) has analysed the way rhyme in poetry is either subordinated to meaning or made coincident with it. He contrasts the rhymes of Pope and Chaucer. Rhyme leads the reader to expect some further similarity between the words which sound the same. In fact, Pope's couplets tend to rhyme words which are different parts of speech (for example 'eyes'/'rise'), and/or syllable length ('laws'/'applause'). We anticipate similarity and find difference:

> Pope's rhymes are characterized by difference in parts of speech or in function of the same parts of speech, the difference in each case being accentuated by the tendency of his couplets to parallel structure. (1970, pp. 157–8)

Such rhyming works to throw a stress upon the meaning so that meaning dominates sound and the rhyme is subordinated. The more exact the rhyme, the greater this effect. Typical rhymes from Chaucer are called 'tame' by Wimsatt because 'the same parts of speech are used in closely parallel functions' (p. 160):

> And he was clad in cote and hood of grene.
> A sheef of pecock arwes, bright and kene . . .

Such rhymes treat the signifier not as subordinate to the signified but rather as in a relationship of equality with it, so that they tend to coincide. Relative to subordination, coincidence in rhyme emphasizes the phonetic, so acknowledging the dependence of signified or signifier. In coincident rhyme meaning is allowed to follow sound as much as sound does meaning; and the less *exact* the rhyme, the greater this effect, for example when only the vowels in the rhyme words have the same sound. 'Bad' rhyme draws attention to the phonetic, as it does in this couplet from a punk song of 1977:

> I'm in love
> With a girl I oughtn't of.

Coincident rhyme foregrounds the signifier.

All the rhymes in 'Three Ravens' are monosyllabic or 'masculine' rhyme except 'feete'/'keepe' (and then only if the final /e/ is pronounced) and 'gentleman'/'leman' (and this strictly is not rhyme but *homoeoteleuton*, which occurs when two words have the same ending). Four rhymes are between the same parts of speech, 'field'/'shield', 'eagerly'/'nie', 'backe'/'lake', 'prime'/ 'time'. Several are half-rhymes or assonance, 'mate'/'take', 'feete'/'keepe', and possibly 'eagerly'/'nie' as well as 'backe'/ 'lake' (depending on how they were pronounced at the time). Pope's rhymes are like tendentious and non-tendentious jokes in Freud's classification, phonetic play held in relation to the syntagmatic chain. These ballad rhymes are seen as 'tame' or 'bad' because, like the jest ('When is a door . . .') they are offered as a source of pleasure in themselves, as they would be for the 9-year-old cited by the Opies in *The Lore and Language of Schoolchildren* who says of a nonsense verse that 'what's so clever about this is the way it all rhymes' (1967, p. 17).

Throughout 'Three Ravens' there is a foregrounding and insistence upon the material process of enunciation – in the use of four-stress metre (if it is spoken, not sung) and in the concurrence between semantic and phonetic, which brings meaning into parallel with the stanza, the line, the rhyme. In each stanza the first line is repeated three times for formal rather than semantic reasons. And crucially there is the refrain:

> Downe a downe, hay down, hay downe . . .
> With a downe . . .
> With a downe derrie, derrie, derrie, downe, downe . . .

(a line referred to, though not necessarily from this ballad, at the end of Pound's 'Canto 83', 'Down, Derry-down'). In addition to occurring 80 times in the refrain, 8 times in each stanza, 'down' appears three times in the substantive couplets, when the body of the knight is said to be 'downe' in the field, when the hounds 'lie downe' at his feet, and when the doe comes 'downe'. These features take on more significance when the medieval ballad is compared to the discourse that supplants it. The simple repetitions of the refrain in the ballad can be compared with the typical use of refrain in the new tradition. For example, in Wyatt's 'My lute awake!', each of the eight stanzas ends with the phrase 'I have done', yet on each occasion it is held within the syntagmatic chain by taking on a new meaning. In contrast, 'Three Ravens' openly provides play with language, pleasurable treatment of words as things.

While the ballad does not aim for closure in the syntagmatic chain, there is a coherence sustained in the narrative despite its parataxis – the ravens threaten the knight while the other animals protect him, as they should. This coherence offers a position for the ego, but a position that does not try to disavow the way it is brought about – socially, subjectively, linguistically – as an effect of the discourse. 'Three Ravens' acknowledges intersubjectivity. The acknowledgment is made at various levels: in the paratactic structuring of the individual text, which operates by combining units from a common discourse, so that each ballad explicitly takes its place among others; in the use of accentual metre, which invites the speaker to share a common rhythm rather than find out an individual intonation; in the many repetitions of the refrain, which make room for collective speech, for others to join in together. Meaning 'insists' in the linearity of the syntagmatic chain and is the place in discourse where consciousness may appear present to itself. At one level 'Three Ravens' is a literal narrative of supernatural events – birds talk and does bury corpses – but the chain of this narrative is structured across paratactic juxtapositions, these rendering it open to paradigmatic substitutions and to a discourse of the unconscious. The parataxis, with its abrupt and unexplained changes of direction, constantly leaves ideas incomplete and in suspension beneath the syntagmatic chain, unexpressed yet latent. A main example here is the outcome of the ravens' wish. At the same time units can be combined paratactically because they *are* units, vivid, pictorial, self-contained, and so are well adapted to function symbolically as though they were the thing-presentations characterizing the unconscious. The medieval ballad is an example of folklore, and Freud recognized the similarity between folkloric material and dream symbolism:

> this symbolism is not peculiar to dreams, but is characteristic of unconscious ideation, in particular among the people, and it is to be found in folklore, and in popular myths, legends, linguistic idioms, proverbial wisdom and current jokes, to a more complete extent than in dreams. (1977, pp. 467–8)

In the ease with which it can be read at one level as 'unconscious ideation' the ballad shows the dependence of the ego on the process of conscious and unconscious which operates to constitute it as ego.

Finally, 'Three Ravens' exhibits rather than tries to conceal the dependence of the signified on the signifier. This can be seen: in the use of accentual metre, which foregrounds enunciation; in the coincidence between meaning and stanza unit, as well as between meaning and line; in the degree to which rhyme, if not leading to meaning, at least contributes as an equal partner in finding it; in the way words are treated as things in the 'downe derries' of the refrain. The attempt is not to hold enunciation onto enounced but rather to celebrate the work/play of the signifier. Thus, a place for the subject of the enounced is produced but it is exhibited as product of the process of enunciation on which it depends. 'Three Ravens' exemplifies a poetic discourse which offers a *relative* position for the ego, a position produced in acknowledged relationship to a field of forces, social, subjective, linguistic. The poem is openly presented to the reader in the first place as a *poem*, as an act of pleasurable speaking. In contrast the discourse founded at the Renaissance aims first of all to represent an individual speaking.

6
The founding moment

I am as I am and so wil I be

Thomas Wyatt,
Poems from the Devonshire MS

Discourse as 'form' and 'content'

In *The Order of Things* Michel Foucault analyses the huge changes produced in discourse and modes of representation at the time of Renaissance. Although the implications of the account are subtle and far-reaching, it is easy to summarize the broad contrast the book describes. In the feudal conception words were thought to have an inherent link to things, to reality, and Foucault lists four categories of this linkage (resemblance, emulation, analogy, sympathy). As example he cites the way Duret in 1613 talks about Hebrew:

> The horse is named *Sus*, thought to be from the verb *Hasas* . . . and it signifies to rise up, for among all four-footed animals the horse is the most proud and brave. . . . (1970, p. 36)

But from the Renaissance, as Foucault shows, 'Things and words were to be separated from one another' (ibid., p. 43).

To facilitate a separation between words and the reality they might refer to, discourse generally began to aim for transparency – 'form' (signifier and means of representation) came to be radically distinguished from 'content' (signified and the represented). The distinction is implied in the work of Peter Ramus (1515–72), French philosopher and logician, whose *Training in Dialectic* was published in 1546 (see Hawkes 1973, pp.

37–42). While the Aristotelian tradition had divided rhetoric into five activities – invention, disposition, elocution, memory, delivery – Ramus grouped three (invention, disposition, memory) together as *dialectic*, that is, logic; and two (elocution, delivery) as *rhetoric*. With 'form' and 'content' opposed as rhetoric and logic, a discourse may aim at transparency, seeking to render 'form' a merely neutral vehicle for communicating 'content'. So Machiavelli, sometime between 1514 and 1519, dedicates *The Prince* to Lorenzo de' Medici as follows:

> I have not embellished or crammed this book with rounded periods or big, impressive words, or with any blandishment or superfluous decoration of the kind which many are in the habit of using to describe or adorn what they have produced; for my ambition has been either that nothing should distinguish my book, or that it should find favour solely through the variety of its contents and seriousness of its subject matter. (1975, pp. 29–30)

The principle is that decoration (*ornamento*) should be disregarded in favour of supposedly direct access to subject-matter (*subietto*). The same principle is promoted in England in 1605 by Francis Bacon. He urges the need to reform English prose, condemning contemporary tendencies in which

> men began to hunt more after words than matter; more after the choiceness of the phrase, and the round and clean composition of the sentence, and the sweet falling of the clauses, and the varying and illustration of their works with tropes and figures, than after the weight of matter, worth of subject, soundness of argument, life of invention, or depth of judgement. (1951, p. 29)

In contrast, Bacon advocates a mode of discourse in which the means of representation ('words') will be merely a vehicle to communicate the represented ('matter').

At the Renaissance, in ways specific to poetic discourse, poetry also aims to give transparent access to the represented. Typically in poetry the represented consists in the first place of an individual speaking. The bourgeois tradition is founded as the project of imitating spoken intonation in poetry so as to make this effect convincing. Techniques for imitating the individual human voice seem to have been invented in song before they were brought over into poetry. The changing relation of music and words in the period up to 1600 needs to be considered, a complex narrative whose historian is John Stevens (1979).

According to Stevens the thirteenth century in Europe 'was the last in which music and poetry and the dance . . . were naturally one and the same art' (p. 34). In song, music and words followed their own separate and specific ways without 'an emotional connection' between them. However, in the fourteenth century 'the natural and necessary union of music and poetry finally broke up' (p. 35). Each achieved the status of autonomous arts, and this autonomy became the basis for a new relationship between them. From now on in song words and meaning dominate music. The music is treated as a kind of ornament or addition to the 'subject matter' of the words, being made to resemble or imitate meaning in various ways – through the 'stylized reproduction of natural sounds', such as noises of the hunt, and by making the music 'symbolically representative' of ideas in the text so that, for example, reference to Christ being strained on the cross is accompanied by long notes. Crucially, from the fifteenth century this feature of resemblance or iconicity includes 'the imitation in music of human speech' (pp. 35–6).

In the early Tudor song-books of the period 1480–1530 'Not only is the ordinary duration of the syllables in speech copied, but even the intonation of speech in the musical melody' (p. 102). If Wyatt's lyrical poetry was spoken not sung (and Stevens gives good though not conclusive evidence that it was) his poetry may show how far the imitation of 'natural' intonation has been introduced from song into poetry of the court (the ballad was unaffected). Based in the use of iambic pentameter the representation of speech was certainly established by the time of *Tottel's Miscellany* (1557) and it is this mode of poetic discourse that Shakespeare's sonnet sequence consolidates and extends. The sonnets break away 'from the formal and incantatory mode . . . to make the verse a more flexible and transparent medium' (Knights 1964, p. 62).

Shakespeare's 'Sonnet 73'

The sonnet represents an ageing speaker who compares his life first to a tree, then to twilight, then to a fire, each metaphor being worked out in a single sentence. The repetition emphasizes the differences of meaning. Thus the comparison with a tree (part of an annual cycle) is repeated with a difference in the comparison with twilight (part of a diurnal cycle), the comparison between the life of man and the life of nature being sustained into a third term which marks a decisive difference, for man's life is like a fire, a single event. That is: while nature goes round and round and man is part of this cycle, the individual life dies once and for all. The repeated metaphors anticipate this once and for all progress, developing from full light (the tree) to twilight (the sunset) and darkness (the fire), from yellow (the leaves), pale red (the fading sunset) to full red (the fire) and grey-white (the ashes). In sum the poem says 'I am growing older every year, every day, every hour (though am not as old as you, young man, may think me) and will inevitably die; but this makes – or should make – you love me all the more while you've still got me'. (For a more detailed account, see Nowottny 1965, pp. 76–87.)

In the Quarto text of 1609, the first published form, the sonnet appears as:

THat time of yeeare thou maist in me behold,
When yellow leaues, or none, or few doe hange
Vpon those boughes which shake against the could,
Bare rn'wd quiers, where late the sweet birds sang.
In me thou seest the twil-light of such day,
As after Sun-set fadeth in the West,
Which by and by blacke night doth take away,
Deaths second self that seals vp all in rest.
In me thou seest the glowing of such fire,
That on the ashes of his youth doth lye,
As the death bed, whereon it must expire,
Consum'd with that which it was nurrisht by.
This thou perceu'st, which makes thy loue more strong,
To loue that well, which thou must leaue ere long.

('rn'wd quiers' in l. 4 is printed by most modern editors as 'ruined choirs'.)

'Sonnet 73' consists of four sentences scrupulously developed and subordinated in structure. There is close parallelism between the first three, not only in the tense and person of the main verbs ('maist . . . behold', 'seest', 'seest') but throughout. The object of each main verb is qualified by relatives ('THat time . . . When', 'such day, As', 'such fire, That') introducing a subordinate clause which contains a further relative clause ('which shake', 'which . . . blacke night', 'whereon'); each is closed by a phrase in apposition ('Bare rn'wd quiers . . .', 'Deaths second self . . .', 'Consum'd . . .'); and further each apposition includes a further relative clause ('where late . . .', 'that seals . . .', 'which it was . . .'). The final couplet, as Roger Fowler shows (1975, p. 106) is ambiguous and 'This' may refer back to the preceding 12 lines or forward to the rest of the couplet, though the meaning is almost the same either way.

The syntagmatic chain is not the same as syntax, for it operates both within the sentence and across sentences as discourse. In the ballad syntax consisted of basic sentence types generally in parataxis:

> There were three rauens sat on a tree,
> They were as blacke as they might be.

This promoted a loose and 'open' syntagmatic chain. Here the syntax supports firm linearity in the chain, for it is strongly recursive, stringing phrases and basic sentences together hierarchically, 'THat time . . . When . . . which . . . where late'. It has 'an ostentatious air of exactitude about it', the accumulation of relative and appositional clauses acting 'as if to make the focus ever more precise' (Fowler 1975, p. 104). Though anticipated semantically (what will be the end of this once and for all progress?), closure is postponed, making the demand for it more insistent. The demand is answered in the abstract, epigrammatic language of the couplet, and the sonnet closes with authority if not entire conviction.

Attention has been drawn to those points in the sonnet at which progressive development of meaning is dislocated – when the anticipated order (yellow/few/none) is momentarily threatened by the actual order (yellow/none/few) and when 'such' (l. 5) is read initially as though it were 'such a day' and only retrospectively as 'such day' (= 'so much of daylight') (see Booth 1969, pp. 118–30). This kind of analysis begins at the level of '*words*' (Fish 1974, p. 387), with signifier already aligned with signified. It fails to recognize that because of the process of enunciation the syntagmatic chain can never be closed, it can only aim for closure. The disturbances indicated are minimal, though even these are avoided in Augustan poetry. 'Sonnet 73' allows for very little sliding of the signifier over the signified; for example, there is no question that in speaking 'time' in the first line we ought to think of 'thyme'. And where it is admitted that the signifier opens onto a plurality of signifieds (as does 'night' in line 7, which, spoken aloud, suggests 'knight'), these are at once led back into the closure of the chain in a coherent polysemy repeated and confirmed throughout the poem (personified like 'Deaths second self', night becomes a 'blacke (k)night' who can 'take away' something). Closure in the chain – along which meaning 'insists' – makes it possible for the poem to represent someone speaking and so provide a coherent position for the reader as subject of the enounced. The degree of closure can be measured against 'Three Ravens'. The parataxis of that text is structured across a major incoherence, the poem ending without clear closure, with a contradiction in fact since the wish to protect the knight and the wish to destroy him are juxtaposed without resolution.

In the ballad, *discours* (in the form of dialogue between the ravens) took place on the basis of *histoire*, that is within the narrative, while the sonnet in contrast proceeds from the outset as *discours*, 'I' and 'thou', that time '*thou* maist in *me* behold'). Addresser and addressee are specified throughout with 'me' (ll. 1, 5, 9) and 'thou' (ll. 1, 5, 9, 13 twice, 14). The poem opens with one demonstrative ('THat') and the couplet begins with another ('This'). The addresser is located in relation to the look of the addressee, the whole poem turning on 'this is how you may see me'. He is also situated in a temporal present, all the verbs being present-tense except for 'sang', 'Consum'd', 'nurrisht' and probably 'must expire' and 'must leave' which have the force of the future tense. All these 'signs of person' are marks of enunciation; they help to represent the presence of a speaker in the poem, to dramatize an individual voice in the enounced.

The substantiality of this represented speaker is further confirmed in 'Sonnet 73' by means of the *referential effect*, that is, when a speaker *apparently* refers to a reality beyond him or herself. This reality thus becomes an object which, in the usual scenario, guarantees the speaker's existence as a subject. The effect is subtle, and as Barthes shows, depends very much for its effectiveness on the use of irony. In *S/Z* he asserts that 'irony . . . is always *classic* language' (1975, p. 45), language that aims for perfect transparency and direct access to a reality conceived as outside it:

> the ironic code is, in principle, an explicit quotation of what someone has said; however, irony acts as a signpost, and thereby it destroys the multivalence we might expect from quoted discourse. A multivalent text can carry out its basic duplicity only if it subverts the opposition between true and false, if it fails to attribute quotations (even when seeking to discredit them) to explicit authorities, if it flouts all respect for origin. . . . (ibid., p. 44)

Flaubert on the other hand uses an irony 'impregnated with uncertainty' (ibid., p. 140) so that we don't know properly whether it is irony or not. The distinction needs a bit of unpacking. And a short digression on classic irony and the referential effect is needed because they are recurrent features of bourgeois poetic discourse and will reappear in later examples.

Irony is conventionally defined as 'saying one thing to mean another' and so rests on a contrast between 'apparent' and 'real' meaning. Sarcasm is the extreme form of irony in which the apparent meaning is opposite to the real one, when I say 'Another lovely day' while it is pouring with rain. If in the same situation I say 'Not as nice as it could be' this is irony (broad rather than fine) for the apparent meaning is 'acceptable but not pleasant weather' while the real meaning is 'it is unpleasantly wet'. Barthes calls the apparent meaning 'quotation' because out of context 'Not as nice as it could be' is multivalent (who is saying it about what?). In ironic use it is fixed as univocal, simply the ironic equivalent of 'it is unpleasantly wet' and so a matter of 'true or false'.

In the example my irony would be hard to mistake because I

would be referring to an everyday object present in actuality. In other instances when the situation referred to is more abstract, irony can be missed. Is the statement 'The Thatcher government is not the best we've ever had' ironic or not? It depends how the sentence is read. If read ironically with a real meaning 'The Thatcher government is bad', the quotation is attributed to the definite intention of a speaker about a definite state of affairs. It has an origin in a subject mutually defined by reference to an object. The context can give powerful though never conclusive evidence of irony, as it might for the Thatcher example in a solidly anti-Tory newspaper. Hence Colin MacCabe offers this definition:

> Classical irony is established in the distance between the original sentence and the sentence as it should be, given the knowledge of reality that the text has already conferred on us. (1978, pp. 17–18)

The 'original' sentence is the apparent meaning and the sentence 'as it should be' is the real meaning. The distinction apparent/real can only occur if the sentence is read ironically, that is as clear reference to a situation. So irony aims for transparency and produces the referential effect.

Irony cannot be finally proved. In 'Sonnet 73' the auxiliary in the first verb, 'thou maist', makes the assertion 'hypothetical' according to Fowler (1975, p. 109). Thus 'you see how old and near to death I am' may be the apparent meaning while the real meaning is 'because you are young you see me as very old when I am only middle-aged'. Some critics have read the sonnet 'straight', Leishman asserting that its author seems to 'have been at least in his nineties' (1968, p. 141), Wilson Knight denying that Shakespeare could 'have been so old as that' (1955, p. 71). If it is read ironically (as I think it should be) the effect is to refer to a real state of affairs and so guarantee the reality of the speaker. The reader is offered a centre around which the poem is to be held in place. 'Three Ravens' provided no such point of origin. The closing wish

> God send euery gentleman,
> Such haukes, such hounds, and such a leman

is very uncertain. It could be 'straight', if pronounced from sympathy with the obedience of hawks, hounds and leman; ironic, if from a point of identification with the ravens, in which case the real meaning is that the gentleman is going to *need* the protection.

It was argued that the ballad gives open precedence to the signifier and acknowledges itself as a text, a moment in the process of enunciation. So also, it may be asserted, does the Shakespeare sonnet, since its use of rhetoric and an elaborately rhyming verse-form serve to emphasize the enunciation which brings into existence the enounced and the represented speaker.

'Rhetoric', as C. S. Lewis says,

> is the greatest barrier between us and our ancestors. . . . Nearly all our older poetry was written and read by men to whom the distinction between poetry and rhetoric, in its modern form, would have been meaningless. (1954, p. 61)

The intertextuality of 'Sonnet 73' explicitly declares the poem's place in the rhetorical tradition. The sonnet reworks a passage from Book 15 of Ovid's *Metamorphoses* (ll. 199–213) while lines 5–8 make use of lines 186–90 from the same book (which was translated by Golding in 1567). The poem is saturated with rhetorical figures, most obviously in the use of *parison* (repetition), such as 'in me behold' and 'In me thou seest' (ll. 5 and 9), or in detail in the use of *polyptoton* by which 'leaves' (l. 2) reappears with a difference as 'leave' in the last line. Formally the text announces itself as poetic discourse by virtue of being a sonnet in a sequence which rejoins – a little late in the day – the Elizabethan sonnet tradition. And the sonnet verse-form, here three quatrains rhyming *abab cdcd efef* and concluded by a couplet, is in the first place an entirely material organization of the text at the phonetic level.

Both rhetoric and rhyme-scheme in the sonnet may seem to acknowledge the precedence of the signifier in a way similar to that described in the case of the ballad. However, such effects do not operate in isolation. It should be remembered that the process of enunciation is ineluctable and always present in any form of discourse. What defines a discourse is the *role accorded* to enunciation in it. In this respect 'Three Ravens' and 'Sonnet 73' exemplify entirely different discourses. Whereas the ballad allowed priority to the process of enunciation, 'Sonnet 73' aims for a closure in the syntagmatic chain which will foreground the enounced and so dominate the process of enunciation. It seeks to emphasize the poem as meaning rather than as language. This can be seen in the use of rhyme.

Supported by the iambic metre, linear coherence in the sonnet is sustained punctiliously, the sense running on from line to line within the quatrain. This produces in an exemplary instance the run-on across the line boundary 'doe hange/Vpon those boughes'. Of the seven rhymes, all are exact and four are between different parts of speech in contrasted functions ('behold'/'could', 'day'/'away', 'fire'/'expire', 'lye'/'by'). In Chapter 5 rhymes were distinguished on the basis of coincidence and subordination. In these terms – and in decisive contrast to the ballad – the rhymes of 'Sonnet 73' exhibit subordination. In them the pleasure of treating words as things is mastered and held in place by the coherence of the syntagmatic chain. This attempted dominance of signifier by signified can be seen in the overall structure of the sonnet. The repetitions making the three quatrains parallel may seem an example of the incremental repetition of the ballad. But while, typically, incremental repetition consists of close repetition leading to abrupt transition in the final term, here the meaning unfolds across the repetitions of the quatrains, these serving mainly to increase the demand for closure answered in the couplet. In the ballad there is a relation of coincidence between signifier and signified which foregrounds enunciation. In contrast, the sonnet tries to *contain* the fact of enunciation by holding it in close relation to meaning, attempting – impossibly – to make the signifier a part of the signified. Instead of coincidence between signifier and signified there is *iconicity*, a feature which persists throughout the bourgeois discourse and so needs introduction now, at its founding moment.

The American logician, Charles Peirce, distinguishes in his analysis of signs between symbol, icon, and index. A symbol, such as a word, has an arbitrary relation to the object it signifies; an icon, such as a painted portrait, resembles its object; an index is a sign because of its causative relation to what it signifies (smoke is the indexical sign of fire). Since, on Saussure's showing, the bond between signifier and signified is conventional only, there being no reason in nature why a horse should be called 'horse' rather than 'equus', it would seem that language can never be iconic. Perhaps this view needs to be qualified. As Jakobson has suggested, there is some general diagrammatic resemblance between language and the rest of the world – plurals are often larger than singulars, and in various Indo-European languages comparative and superlative degrees of adjectives show 'a gradual increase in the number of phonemes, e.g., *high*, *higher*, *highest*, . . .' (1965, p. 29). But such generalized resemblances in language would never allow a reader to pass from the phonetic to the semantic without knowing the language in question. And there is broad acceptance (see Leech 1969, pp. 96–100; Traugott and Pratt 1980, pp. 69–71, and Attridge 1981) of the view put forward by Shapiro and Beum that iconicity in poetic discourse can only be perceived in a reverse movement from the semantic to the phonetic. Sounds have a range of *potential* iconicity but this is only latent:

> The semantic content of words has to activate and focus this imitative potential. If the semantic element does not do this, then the collocations of sounds are in most cases merely neutral. (Shapiro and Beum 1965, p. 15)

The reader who does not know Latin may test this on Vergil's line

> quadripedante putrem sonitu quatit ungula campum.
> (*Aeneid* VIII. 596)

Its iconic effect emerges only if we know we should look for a phonetic version of the idea of horses galloping.

Within the deliberately vague concept of resemblance it is useful to distinguish three forms of iconicity, two produced by intonation and one which is phonetic. Intonation is iconic if it is perceived as resembling a phenomenon described, as in the line from Vergil. Another example, one cited by the Belgian critics 'Group Mu' from Eliot's 'Preludes', is the line 'A lonely cab-horse steams and stamps' in which, they say, 'the regular iambic verse puts the two terms under the same stress' ('steams and stamps') so that there is an 'evocation of stamping' (1977, p. 151). Intonation is also iconic when the phenomenon the poetry seeks to imitate is the intonation of the spoken voice. This has been considered already in relation to iambic pentameter and also through the earlier discussion of the influence of song on Renaissance lyric poetry.

A third and important form of iconicity uses the phonetic properties of language to set up resemblance to a phenomenon, so that the sound is felt to 'expess' or 'enact' the sense. The effect is not magic but can be explained in terms of *protosemanticism*. This term refers to the fact that some semantic potential attaches even to single phonemes and clusters of phonemes, so making them available for iconic exploitation. According to Geoffrey Leech it is 'possible to list classes of English consonants impressionistically on a scale of increasing hardness' (1969, p. 98) from liquids and nasals (/l/, /r/, etc.) to plosives (/b/, /d/, etc.). The potential increases when single phonemes are combined. Counter-instances such as 'snake', 'snip', and 'snack' notwithstanding, Nelson Francis is surely right to note that in English there is 'an association between the initial consonant cluster *sn-* and the nose (snarl, sneer, sneeze, sniff, snivel, snore . . .)' (1965, p. 162). On Eliot's line Group Mu add that the idea of stamping, aided by the rhythm, 'brings into relief the protosemanticism of /st/ (stay, stand, stop, stress . . .)' (1977, p. 151). Protosemanticism is also remarked by Francis in the final *-er* on verbs which can suggest 'rapidly repeated, often rhythmic motion, as in *flicker*, *flutter*, *hover* . . .' (1965, p. 162). Such protosemanticism begins to explain where and how the 'imitative potential' for iconicity can be found.

It is important to stress, as does Attridge (1981), that iconicity exists as it is perceived, and so is historically – that is ideologically – instituted along with the expectations surrounding aesthetic discourse generally and poetic discourse specifically. It is hard to say how much of the 'flat' and 'uninflected' quality a modern reader may feel about 'Three Ravens' is due to its relative failure to answer a demand for iconicity:

> The one of them said to his mate,
> 'Where shall we our breakefast take?'

In this there is little more correspondence between meaning and sound than ensues for language in general from the diagrammatic resemblances Jakobson points to. The example of song makes it easier to grasp the idea of positive non-correspondence between the 'parts' of an aesthetic text, in this case non-correspondence between words and music. 'If musical logic demanded' the late medieval composer 'would end a section with a firm cadence half-way through a word, or split a word in two with a long rest' (Trowell 1963, p. 18). The account of Tudor music already summarized makes clear how far iconicity has invaded song by the Renaissance. It also becomes part of poetic discourse, a means to contain enunciation.

Among many iconic effects in the sonnet I shall instance only two, one in rhythm, one in sound. In autumn trees lose their leaves one by one until none are left. A resemblance to this phenomenon can be recognized in the intonation contours of lines 2–3. The speaking voice is forced to move evenly and hesitantly ('leaues, or none, or few') and rise and speed up at the end of the line ('doe hange'). The glide on 'hange' is protracted by the search for a pause at the line ending, then made up for by greater rapidity at the start of the next line ('Vpon those boughes'). This movement – slower and slower, then sudden speed – can be felt to resemble the idea of the gradual isolation of the leaves and their sudden fall. Line 4 ('Bare rn'wd quiers, where late the sweet birds sang') offers a complex pattern of identical and related sounds, especially in the vowels. Easier to analyse is the repetition of sibilants in 'Death*s* *s*econd *s*elf that *s*eals vp all in re*s*t'. The ideas of death, sleep and a black (k)night bring out the protosemantic potential of a sinister connotation in /s/. The line also exemplifies the conditions for such iconicity in rhythm and sound. These effects will be diminished and probably lost unless pronunciation is overcorrected. One /s/ in line 8 disappears if there is an elision into 'Death'second' instead of cessation of phonation. Partly this overcorrection follows from the rhetorical self-consciousness of a text in which, for instance, the reader is expected to note the *polyptoton* 'leaues'/ 'leaue'. However, as was argued earlier (pp. 68–9) the necessary condition for the effect is iambic pentameter, for this requires every syllable to be pronounced.

The major iconicity of 'Sonnet 73' lies in the way its words are made to resemble the speaking of an individual voice. The effect is achieved both positively and negatively. Positively, there has to be firm coherence in the syntagmatic chain, both in detail – so that signified does not slide under signifier – and overall – so that the larger meaning of the text can work towards closure (as it does here in the couplet). 'Sonnet 73' is *discours*, not *histoire*; it bears vivid marks of enunciation. It makes use of the referential effect: the represented speaker refers ironically to some reality behind the apparent meaning of his words, so confirming his reality as a speaker, an 'I' to a reciprocal 'it'. Negatively, the effect of a voice 'actually' speaking has to be defended against what would undermine it by exhibiting how it is produced as an effect. Through a specific 'economy', rhetoric and rhyme are treated so as to rob them of force as enunciation. The process of enunciation cannot be annihilated but it can be held in place, mitigated, disclaimed by such features as the iconicity, this aiming to render signifier subordinate to signified by making it consonant with meaning.

Through coherent representation of a vivid and substantial speaker the poem foregrounds a position for the reader as subject of the enounced while denying his or her position as subject of enunciation. 'Sonnet 73' is a script for the speaking voice, a means to represent someone speaking in the present just as the actor playing Hamlet has an appropriate piece of script to speak sword in hand over the praying Claudius. Here there is a different script but one which equally contrives to give the effect of personal 'presence'. Just as realist cinema uses its means of enunciation, a photographic image and recorded sound, to produce 'real' people in a 'real' story (the enounced), so the sonnet uses appropriately poetic means for a similar purpose. The effect is so realistic that – to take simply one of many examples in conventional criticism of the sonnets – in 'Sonnet 73' 'the reader feels as much addressed as the young man, if not more so' (Hammond 1981, p. 81). Hence the sonnets can be performed 'almost as if Shakespeare were talking to you', speaking 'nakedly as "I"'. While the ballad 'Three Ravens' offers itself as a poem, 'Sonnet 73' offers itself as a 'presence' by disavowing itself as a poem.

In *The Motives of Eloquence*, a book on poetry and Renaissance rhetoric, Richard Lanham distinguishes between two kinds of self, one 'rhetorical', one 'serious'. The rhetorical self is social and playful, founded in language, while the serious one is 'a central self, an irreducible identity' (1976, p. 1). From this basis it is argued that 'Shakespeare's sonnets superpose these two poetics one upon the other' (p. 111). Lanham does not explain this eternal opposition of selves, which concedes a rhetorical self only in order to maintain the absolute integrity of the 'serious' self. Obviously, the theoretical position on discourse and subjectivity outlined above in Chapter 3 denies that the self is in any sense 'irreducible', refuses the eternal opposition between 'social' and 'central', and asserts that both 'selves' are effects of discourse and should be grasped in Lacan's terms of the Symbolic and the Imaginary.

The 'superposition' Lanham discerns in the sonnets can be better understood as, on the one hand, the promotion (by the text) of a coherent position for the subject of the enounced by means of the plausible representation of 'presence' or 'central self'; and, on the other, the containment (by the text) of enunciation, rhetoric and the play of language. A speaker for 'Sonnet 73' is represented with such powerful realism that he seems to lie behind the rhetoric, using it as though from a point beyond language. The text has 'Shakespearian life' in the sense Leavis has defined it, 'as if the words as words withdrew themselves from the focus of our attention and we were directly aware of a tissue of feelings and perceptions' (1967, p. 47). And the reader is invited into identification with this 'presence' supposedly experienced directly and without words.

Nevertheless, the rhetoric and especially the sonnet form itself is still there. As contrast with subsequent developments in the discourse makes clear, the position offered to the reader in 'Sonnet 73' is not fully transcendental, that is, not one which denies entirely its own production. For all the containment, the rhetoric remains to acknowledge a dependence on enunciation, even if the represented speaker can be envisaged as 'using' a rhetoric that does not include him. The sonnet marks a radical break with the feudal form of discourse exemplified by 'Three Ravens'. But in 1600 the new discourse still carries with it residual elements that are eliminated in the early seventeenth century (for this argument made with reference to a Milton sonnet, see Easthope 1981). The ideal of wholly transparent language for poetry only becomes explicit after 1660.

7
Transparency as explicit ideal

Expression is the *Dress* of *Thought*

Pope,
'Essay on Criticism'

The Augustan programme

Whatever local commitments it took on during the revolutionary period, after 1660, as Stanley Fish asserts, 'the plain style wins the day' (1974, p. 379). It does so with a self-conscious programme and a belief that reality simply exists unproblematically outside and prior to discourse. Accordingly, a discourse, including a poetic discourse, has only to avoid wordiness and it can give direct access to reality as though through a clear window. Dryden's 'Preface' to 'Religio Laici' (1682) advocates a 'Plain and Natural' style through which instruction about objects can 'be given by shewing them what they naturally are' (1962, p. 282). The principle extends to satire for, in the well known passage, good satire is distinguished from bad on this basis: instead of calling names, 'rogue and villain', it *shows* by making 'a man appear a fool, a blockhead, or a knave' (Dryden, 1967/68, vol. 2, p. 136).

Reality is simply *there* to be referred to by discourse, and so discourse must make itself transparent so that it can refer: the classic announcement of this ideal is in Thomas Sprat's *History of the Royal Society* (1667):

> the resolution of the Royal Society has been . . . to reject all amplifications, digressions, and swellings of style; to return back to the primitive purity and shortness, when men de-

> liver'd so many *things* almost in an equal number of *words*. They have extracted from all their members a close, naked, natural way of speaking, positive expressions, clear senses, a native easiness, bringing all things as near the Mathematical plainness as they can, and preferring the language of Artizans, Countrymen, and Merchants, before that of Wits or Scholars. (1908, II, pp. 117–18)

Sprat assumes an atomistic and unitary correlation between discourse and reality, 'so many *things*, almost in an equal number of *words*'. The sentence is thought to be merely the sum of its component words (and the 'things' they 'deliver'). But as Stephen Land describes, from the time of Hobbes on into the next century the individual word is 'slowly replaced as the unit of significance by the sentence' (1974, p. v). From a study of ideas about language put forward in theories of universal language, grammars and shorthand systems, Murray Cohen arrives at a similar conclusion:

> In the last quarter of the seventeenth century, there were noticeable shifts in attitudes towards language. . . . By the beginning of the eighteenth century, the idea of language study had shifted from the taxonomic representation of words and things to the establishment of the relationship between speech and thought. Seventeenth-century linguists sought to establish an isomorphic relationship between language and nature; in the early eighteenth century, linguists assumed that language reflects the structure of the mind. (1977, pp. xxiii–iv)

The development in short is from an empiricist to a rationalist conception of the relation between discourse and reality.

Accordingly, within discourse, the effect of transparency depends not so much on the individual word as on linear coherence in the syntagmatic chain. This is what Hobbes recommends for the sentence (the 'period') and for word order:

> For the order of words, when placed as they ought to be, carries a light before it, whereby a man may foresee the length of his period, as a torch in the night shews a man the stops and unevenness in his way. But when plac'd unnaturally, the Reader will often find unexpected checks, and be forced to go

> back and hunt for the sense, and suffer such unease, as in a Coach a man unexpectedly finds in passing over a furrow. (1908, II, p. 69)

Discourse here is conceived explicitly as direct communication, a vehicle to transport the reader smoothly to the meaning without drawing attention to itself. The Augustan ideal of transparency is advanced in such terms as 'clear', 'natural', 'easy'. But since, as ever, there can be no signified without a signifier, another set of terms points to the 'decorum' in which signifier is to be held onto signified ('fit', 'proper', 'apt'). Genre is one mode of this containment. The principle is that 'diff'rent *Styles* with diff'rent *Subjects* sort' (Pope's 'Essay on Criticism', l. 322) and that an economy operating across texts should regulate differences of language by making texts always the same in so far as there is always the same generic mediation between subject matter and style ('low' subject, so 'low' style, etc.). This is one way in which, in the pervasive common-place, language is to be the dress of thought. Enunciation is still acknowledged in rhetoric and rhyme. But the traditional schemes, tropes, and figures of rhetoric are firmly subordinated to meaning. And in the couplet the poet is urged to contrive the sense 'into such words that the rhyme shall naturally follow them, not they the rhyme' (Dryden 1967/68, I, p. 8). In Augustan theory 'form' and 'content' are recognized as irredeemably separate, yet the wish is to make 'form' adhere to 'content' as closely as clothes fit the body, so becoming an autonomous source of pleasure as an appropriate and civilized artifice. These features can be exemplified in a passage from 'The Rape of the Lock'.

From Pope's 'The Rape of the Lock'

In the narrative of the poem Belinda is a victim on whom the Baron, supported by Clarissa, seeks to impose castration by cutting off a lock of her hair. The poem itself regards Belinda as an uncertain object which needs to be fixed in place and mastered, a mystery to be penetrated, resolved and known. The poem, then, follows the classic empiricist project of trying to discern the real meaning behind Belinda's appearance. Central to this project is the description of Belinda on a barge taking her to Hampton Court.

Canto II begins:

> Not with more Glories, in th'Etherial Plain,
> The Sun first rises o'er the purpled Main,
> Than issuing forth, the Rival of his Beams
> Lanch'd on the Bosom of the Silver *Thames*.
> Fair Nymphs, and well-drest Youths around her shone,
> But ev'ry Eye was fix'd on her alone.
> On her white Breast a sparkling *Cross* she wore,
> Which *Jews* might kiss, and Infidels adore.
> Her lively Looks a sprightly Mind disclose,
> Quick as her Eyes, and as unfix'd as those:
> Favours to none, to all she Smiles extends,
> Oft she rejects, but never once offends.
> Bright as the Sun, her Eyes the Gazers strike,
> And, like the Sun, they shine on all alike.
> Yet graceful Ease, and Sweetness void of Pride,
> Might hide her Faults, if *Belles* had Faults to hide:
> If to her share some Female Errors fall,
> Look on her Face, and you'll forget 'em all.

Unlike that of 'Sonnet 73', the syntax of this passage is not organized in a complex hierarchy of subordination, but it is considerably varied. The couplet form, which dictates so much in Augustan poetry, generally precludes sentences more than two lines long (1–4 here are an exception). Most sentences in the passage are co-ordinated ('But ev'ry Eye . . .', 'but never once', 'And, like the Sun . . .'), one is subordinated with a relative ('Which *Jews* . . .'), and the passage ends with two conditional clauses ('if *Belles* . . .', 'If to her share . . .'). Elsewhere in Pope a quite different kind of syntax can be found, for example in the portrait of Atticus where it parodies Addison's own syntactic style. Syntax shows local variation. Like word-order, which is frequently inverted, in this passage it decorates and confirms the description of Belinda. Syntax is available for iconic purposes because meaning is strongly sustained at a 'deeper' level along the syntagmatic chain. The comparison of Belinda to the sun leads via the reference to the cross on which the sun shines to the shining of Belinda's eyes and so to the question of how far the intentions implied by her outward behaviour are consistent with her inner intentions, a question which achieves partial closure in the ironic summary of the last four lines but is passed on for answer in the narrative of the poem as a whole. The individual couplets are strung like beads on a syntagmatic chain which aims for complete closure. Contrast with 'Sonnet 73' tends to confirm Land's account of how discourse had developed since 1609: in Shakespeare the sentence and the syntagmatic chain were close to being the same thing while in Pope the chain is sustained not so much in the sentence as at the level of the whole utterance.

The strict linearity of the chain not only works to hold signifier punctiliously onto signified but also seeks to include in its coherence any play of meaning and slide of the signifier. In line 4 'Bosom' and 'Silver' are gathered up in the idea of the cross on the breast in line 7, and a similar play on 'fix'd'/'unfix'd' is *thematized*, that is, made part of the meaning, as the contrast between how she is looked at and how she looks back. In fact, a main effect of the passage, the irony, tends to turn almost every reference into a kind of tendentious joke and so into a play of words held in place by semantic purpose. For example, when the nymphs and youths are said to shine, the apparent meaning is that they are attractive and brilliant while the real meaning is that they merely pretend to brilliance in contrast to the sun, which possesses it by nature. So there is a play between at least two meanings in 'shone' and both are thematized, that is, made relevant to the overall sense. However, this is a good point to recall that because of the process of enunciation the syntagmatic chain can *never* be entirely closed. The signifier always slides and produces an excess of meaning. This can be exemplified simply by testing the passage for homonyms. There is no relevant sense in which the reader should think of a son or even the Son of God at the words 'The Sun first rises . . .' (though this play is possible, e.g. Shakespeare's 'Sonnet 33') and it is doubtful whether the rivalry between the sun and Belinda is meant to be a matter of his being 'first' while she comes fourth ('issuing forth'). Such play, too close to the childish vulgarity of the jest, is not meant to happen here. That between 'Eye' and 'I' is probably thematized if only because it always is; whether there should be any move from '*Belles*' to 'bells' is impossible to decide. There is no way the syntagmatic chain can entirely exclude such play, stop a reader thinking of Belles as bells. It can only disavow it, pretend it doesn't happen, and work to gather in what it can of the inevitable excess.

The passage, and indeed the poem, is mainly addressed to us as *histoire* with an implied narrator. But the narrator turns into a represented speaker in the course of the description when he (it is a he) takes on marks of enunciation. In fact it shows how easily the modes of *discours* and *histoire* can be transposed. The narration begins in the past tense ('lanch'd') but moves into the present at 'disclose' (l. 9) and finally emerges unequivocally as *discours* with an imperative ('Look') and second person pronoun in line 18. The presence of the speaker – or rather the narrator/represented speaker – is solidly established by the constant use of irony and so of the referential effect. This is pervasive, an obvious example being the innuendo:

> On her white Breast a sparkling *Cross* she wore,
> Which *Jews* might kiss, and Infidels adore.

Innuendo can be defined as irony concerning a sexual topic in which the apparent meaning remains polite. Here the (tendentious) joke is produced by play between whether the antecedent of 'Which' is 'breast' or 'cross'. In the apparent meaning, men are persuaded to kiss her cross and in the real meaning they kiss her breast. The whole passage depends on an ironic mock-heroic comparison between Belinda and the sun. The apparent meaning is that she is a heroine of epic seriousness who deserves an epic simile ('Not with more . . .'). In ironic contrast to this is the real meaning that she is an ordinary woman in a contemporary society and not heroic at all. However, there is a double irony, for this becomes itself an apparent meaning to the real implication that Belinda is after all like the sun since, in the tradition of courtly love, she is sunlike in virtue of her beauty. The final couplet appears to offer gallantry, a compliment to Belinda's beautiful face:

> If to her share some Female Errors fall,
> Look on her Face, and you'll forget 'em all.

Irony can always be disputed and at least one critic finds this a 'straightforward ringing declaration' (Jones 1969, p. 100). But behind this apparent meaning a real meaning can be discovered, namely, that the beauty of Belinda's face should *not* make you forget about her moral qualities. Even if the nature of the relation between Belinda's behaviour and her moral intentions is not certain, the existence of the relation itself is unmistakable. And as this relation becomes an object supposedly referred to 'out there', the narrator becomes firmly established as a subject. As discussed in the previous chapter, this is the referential effect which treats language as transparent. The omnipresence of the irony and its certainty relative to that in 'Sonnet 73' suggest how far the discourse had progressed by the early eighteenth century, progressed, that is, in trying to give supposedly unmediated access to a reality it purports to represent.

The enounced of a discourse is only brought about by enunciation, and though separated off as 'form' as against 'content', enunciation can be held onto content. An economy of containment, established with the founding of the discourse, is pushed further in the Augustan period through an iconicity more consistent and inclusive than that of 'Sonnet 73'. Dryden's explicit principle that 'propriety of sound' is 'to be varied according to the nature of the subject' (1967/68, II, p. 40) is extended in Pope: 'a good Poet will adapt the very Sounds, as well as Words, to the Things he treats of' (1956, I, p. 107). Iconicity now aims to comprehend sound, intonation, syntax and word order.

Examples of phonetic iconicity are already familiar in criticism of Pope and I do not mean to cite more than one from this passage, the fact that the /l/ sounds of 'lively Looks' can be perceived as appropriate for Belinda's animated glances. Such phonetic effects can take on precise definition because the pronunciation is to be even more fastidious than in Shakespeare. Details of phonetic repetition and variation are much more carefully patterned in Pope, so making more phonemes and morphemes available for semanticization. The /k/ in 'Looks' repeats a similar sound from 'sparkling', '*Cross*' and 'kiss', helping to lend the sound of 'Looks' a meaning from its association with the idea of the cross, the kiss, and so the breast. Intonational iconicity also occurs throughout, and is hard to separate from that produced phonetically. Thus, in the same example, the semantic similarity between Belinda's looks and her mind is made iconic by the rhythmic similarity between 'lively Looks' and 'sprightly Mind', both adjectives ending '-ly', the first phrase bound together with alliteration, the second with assonance ('spright-', 'Mind').

When contrasted with 'Sonnet 73' the passage shows a considerable innovation in the way syntax and word-order – and so necessarily intonation – are exploited for iconic purposes. Sentences and phrases occur typically in parallel, in antithesis, or as the combination of both in *chiasmus* ('Favours to none, to all she Smiles extends'). For example, the contrast between Belinda as one of the crowd and Belinda as a focus of attention can be seen as imitated by the syntax, intonation and word-order:

> Fair Nymphs, and well-drest Youths around her shone,
> But ev'ry Eye was fix'd on her alone.

The effect depends on the co-ordinated syntax and the way the intonation of the couplet gives such prominence to the word 'fix'd'.

The effect also depends on word-order, which is inverted to 'place' Belinda along with the crowd ('Youths around her shone') to an extent that she would not be in the normal prose order ('youths shone around her'). This feature of Augustan poetry has often been noticed and doesn't need more exemplification here. The two main explanations for it do deserve emphasis. It can only happen because the poetic discourse is still committed to rhetoric and so to formal patterns in enunciation, particularly that brought about by inversion in word-order. This, as will be argued, is founded in the use of the heroic couplet. Second, syntax and word-order are free to be worked iconically because of the firm linearity of the syntagmatic chain running across the couplets. The aim is not to foreground or display enunciation but rather to contain it by semanticizing it, by making it adhere to meaning.

A similar principle holds for the use of rhyme, as has been suggested earlier. Wimsatt asserts that 'Pope's couplets . . . tend to hover on the verge of antithesis' (1970, p. 159), while Jones finds this view doubtful and claims that in 'at least half of Pope's couplets' there is a parallel in meaning between the first and second lines, so that the rhyme supports the meaning rather than being contrasted with it (1969, p. 8). Of nine rhymes from the passage in Canto II five link different, four link similar parts of speech. But in either case the syntagmatic chain rides across and dominates any phonetic similarity in the rhyme words. The situation with the rhyme is well summarized by Hugh Kenner, though in terms of Pope's supposed intentions:

> He means us, when we are reading lines of his, to be visited by no suspicion that the first rhyme of a pair has suggested the second, or *vice versa*: to judge rather that the rhyme validates a structure of meaning which other orders of cogency have produced. (1980, p. 67)

Words must not be treated as things, able to lead to meaning. Sound must either be rendered iconic, so as to echo sense, or where it is not, as in some rhymes, the pleasure of the sound must be thoroughly subordinated to meaning.

The question then becomes, as Wimsatt puts it in another essay ('Rhetoric and Poems'), why 'verse basically ordered by the rational rules of parallel and antithesis' should rely so much 'on so barbarous and Gothic a device as rhyme?' (1970, pp. 182–3). His reply, that poets don't always practice what they preach, solves nothing, and I shall try to give a better answer. It is one that cannot draw too much on the passage from Canto II. When Leigh Hunt attacked the 'monotony and uniformity' of the heroic couplet in 1814, he took these lines as evidence of the 'kind of sing-song' he was against – the caesura often occurs in the same place and several lines repeat the standard variation of beginning with a stressed syllable. In citing Hunt's view, Winifred Nowottny has argued that the metrical 'monotonies of this passage' are contrived as 'a metrical equivalent to Belinda's indifference' (1972, p. 8). If this is so, then details of the metre here are a local effect, another aspect of the iconicity.

The rhyme is there so that there can be heroic couplets, the couplet being the form of line organization in which all other aspects of the Augustan style are grounded. Like iambic pentameter and indeed like discourse itself, the couplet is determined in three ways at once: linguistically, ideologically, subjectively.

The linguistic shape of the couplet can be considered first. In 'high' Augustan practice the couplet becomes even more closed than it was earlier. Dryden's verse admits triplet rhymes, the occasional hexameter (or alexandrine) and frequent use of run-on lines, all of which are avoided in Pope. The line becomes end-stopped and with a firm caesura, for as Pope claims, 'in any smooth English verse of ten syllables, there is naturally a *Pause* at the fourth, fifth, or sixth syllable' (cited Tillotson 1962, p. 117). The verse form therefore prescribes a very high degree of isomorphism between phonetic, syntactic and semantic elements. The line (and so intonation) coincides with: (1) the phonetic as represented by sound in the rhymes; (2) the syntax as closed at line ending and couplet ending, and dictated by caesura; (3) meaning, which generally is completed inside the two lines.

The heroic couplet operates the same economy as pentameter but in a more extreme definition. On the one hand, the abstract pattern is more rigidly and uniformly prescribed, since there is the isomorphism of phonetic, syntactic and semantic elements. On the other hand, as Jakobson has noted, intonation is very important 'in poems like "The Rape of the Lock"' (1960, p. 365). The couplet promotes a peculiarly Augustan intonation in the way the second line completes and answers the first. A high tonal rise on the first rhyme word corresponds to a low fall on the second, giving the 'sing-song' of which Leigh Hunt complained. This breadth of tonal contrast, typically greater than in unrhymed iambic pentameter, provides for a greater and more discriminated range of tone. There is the same counterpoint effect of pentameter but in a more contrasted economy, a greater rigidity of pattern *together with* a more fine discrimination in the intonation.

The couplet form is ideologically significant, its rhyming uniformity having strong connotations of order, as has often been noted. In 1694 Dryden writes that rhyme 'bounds' what would otherwise be 'wild and lawless' (1967/68, vol. 1, p. 8), and it is in this spirit that Christopher Caudwell (for example) says that after the blank verse of the Civil War period, poetry between 1650 and 1688 'indicates its readiness to compromise by moving within the bounds of the heroic couplet' (1946, p. 118). The couplet is able to produce a sense of closed order, not only because of the repeated uniformity of the rhyme scheme, but also because each couplet anticipates a closure in which the second line answers the first. Even a first line which is a complete sentence (e.g. l. 7 in the passage) is rendered incomplete by the expectation set up from the couplet form, as though dots were inserted so that it read 'On her white Breast a sparkling *Cross* she wore . . . Which *Jews*, etc.'.

The couplet is fundamental to the operation by which Augustan poetry produces a position for the subject. Although the success of the Romantic revolution for us now tends to make all Augustan poetry seem stylized and artificial, nevertheless the couplet positively encourages rather than impedes the aim of transparency. It does so by working to strengthen the distinction between 'form' and 'content'. Relative to the Renaissance verse-forms which preceded it, Augustan poetry eradicates complex rhyme schemes in favour of the couplet. The tactic is as it were to make the best of a bad job. Granted that the phonetic level is always there and that enunciation is inescapable, the couplet tries to deal with it at a stroke by gathering all enunciation into the single uniformity of the rhyme. The effect is to separate off enunciation as 'form'. At the same time the couplet is able to act as a powerfully syntagmatic force, sustaining 'content'. This is because the very uniformity of the couplet, constantly repeated, tends to make it invisible except as a sign for continuation, as is well explained by Barbara Herrnstein Smith in *Poetic Closure*:

> Although it may seem paradoxical, the 'closed couplet' may be just as strong a force for formal continuity as the open couplet, . . . all those conditions which produce closure in the individual couplet also increase the integrity of the couplet as a formal unit, so that it tends to function within the poem as a single, though complex, formal element. Thus a succession of closed couplets will have all the characteristics of *any systematic repetition of formal elements*, including . . . its effectiveness in maintaining the reader's expectation of continuation.
>
> (1968, p. 73)

In Augustan practice meaning is developed along the syntagmatic chain across the individual couplets and down the paragraph. In this respect meaning is developed in independence from the verse form, each couplet being treated as a bead strung along the syntagmatic chain which runs through it.

In 'The Rape of the Lock' syntagmatic coherence is the basis for the representation of an unnamed narrator and sometimes speaker who refers ironically to aspects of the scene he describes as though it were clearly visible to him. All of this takes place in the enounced. Meanwhile, the process of enunciation, which makes it possible, is separated off as being merely 'formal', and a series of enunciative features – sound, intonation, word-order, even syntax – are denied in so far as they are held in relation to the enounced by being made iconic. A position is therefore secured for the transcendental ego, transcendental in that it is produced by enunciation but the process of that production is disavowed. The reader is offered identification with the anonymous speaker represented by the poem.

The couplet is a basis for the use of traditional rhetoric in Augustan poetry, particularly inversion of word-order. The couplet requires semantic closure at the line ending; in English few sentences end with a verb, but if word-order is inverted a verb can end the line and add to the number of possible rhyme words. So the couplet fosters such rhetorically formal inversions as 'Favours to none, to all she Smiles extends'. Without the couplet, without rhyme, without word-order inversion, and with rhetoric much reduced a different effect begins to emerge, as can be seen if lines 7–10 from the passage are re-written as follows:

> On her white breast she wore a sparkling cross,
> Which Jews might kiss and infidels would love.
> Her lively looks disclose a sprightly mind,
> Quick as her eyes, and as unfixed as them.

A central innovation of Romanticism is to jettison the couplet so as to gain a more prosaic word-order and syntax, and achieve a more naturalistic effect.

8
The continuities of Romanticism

From the dread watch-tower of man's absolute self

Coleridge,
'To William Wordsworth'

The 'Preface' to 'Lyrical Ballads'

In the 'Preface' (1802) Wordsworth notes the effect on the human mind of social forces 'unknown to former times', including

> the encreasing accumulation of men in cities, where the uniformity of their occupations produces a craving for extraordinary incident, which the rapid communication of intelligence hourly gratifies. (1965, p. 249)

Romantic ideology is a polarizing structure: people react against urbanization, industrialism and the increased division of labour, impersonality in the social world, by pursuing a subjective intensity and wholeness. Poetry takes on a new role as home for such internal creativity. This leads to a newly explicit self-consciousness about poetry, and to manifesto statements such as the 'Preface'. In discussing this and later prose by Eliot and Pound I shall be treating them as useful commentaries, not granting them any special authority. At the same time the quest for 'paradise within' privileges those moments when the distinction between external and internal appears elided, especially in childhood and childhood as it is remembered. One such memory Wordsworth describes by saying:

> I was often unable to think of external things as having external existence, and I communed with all that I saw as something not apart from, but inherent in, my own immaterial nature. (1947, IV, p. 463)

This state, so central to Romanticism, is an extreme version of what Lacan defines as the Imaginary, that is, when the subject appears fully present to itself in a signified without a signifier, a represented without means of representation.

Romantic poetic theory is founded on precisely this misrecognition. It affirms that experience is represented in language but denies any activity of means of representation in producing this represented. This is the case in *Biographia Literaria* and Shelley's *Defence*, and it can be readily illustrated in the 'Preface' to *Lyrical Ballads*. Wordsworth's 'Preface' consistently assumes that language is all but transparent to experience, that the enounced is virtually untrammelled by enunciation. A poet has greater 'power in expressing what he thinks and feels' (1965, p. 256), and transparency inheres in the concept of expression. It does so because expression means that the inward can be made outward without any changes because it passes into it as though through a clear medium. Transparency characterizes both language in general as it is actually used and language in poetry. For the 'Preface' experience exists outside language and prior to signification. It follows that poetry is also transparent to experience – 'poetry is the spontaneous overflow of powerful feelings' (ibid., p. 246). On this basis the 'Preface' is able to identify language in general with poetry: there is no 'essential difference between the language of prose and metrical composition' (ibid., p. 253). So, at a stroke, all the specific forms of enunciation that make poetry poetry are rendered accidental to it. The essence that remains is the represented of actual speech translated directly across as the represented of poetry.

The 'Preface' makes two moves to support this position. In the first, good and bad poetry are discriminated. All poetry in which the forms of enunciation are manifest or at all obvious is defined as bad poetry. Thus the whole tradition for which literature, including poetry, is a form of rhetoric is dismissed.

The 'Preface' does not mention rhetoric by name but it does refer throughout to 'poetic diction' and in the 1802 'Appendix' gives a polemical history of rhetoric as the 'mechanical adoption' of 'figures of speech', 'a motley masquerade of tricks, quaintnesses, hieroglyphics, and enigmas'. With rhetoric identified as bad poetry the way is open to define good poetry as that which lacks not only traditional rhetoric but *any forms of enunciation at all* – 'all good poetry *is* the spontaneous overflow of powerful feelings' (my italics).

But language is always a material process of enunciation, a fact most obviously marked in poetic discourse by its composition in lines, which thus exhibit 'parallelism of the signifier' (Lacan 1977a, p. 155). In its Imaginary misrecognition of language and poetry the 'Preface' disavows the forms of enunciation specific to poetry and in so doing denies what these forms signify. 'Poetry is . . . powerful feelings': the copula is emphatic and polemical. Poetry does not imitate or represent experience, it *is* experience itself.

Yet the position remains almost impossible to defend, and a second set of manoeuvres has to be carried out around it. (1) The 'Preface' tries not to allow that life and art, experience and the poetic representation of experience, are different. Poetry 'must . . . fall far short of that which is uttered by men in real life' (1965, p. 256). But this admits only a difference in degree ('fall short'), not kind. The passage goes on to concede what it must:

> However exalted a notion we would wish to cherish of the character of a Poet, it is obvious, that, while he describes and imitates passions, his situation is altogether slavish and mechanical, compared with the freedom and power of real and substantial action and suffering. (ibid., p. 256)

(2) The concession is made only to be immediately recuperated. Though in comparison with life poetry is 'altogether mechanical' (only 'in some degree mechanical' from the 1845 edition onwards), the poet must try to overcome this if he can, by identifying his actual feelings with those represented by the characters in his poetry. (3) Even so, a residue of the 'mechanical', of the material process of enunciation, stays unaccounted for: poetry is written in lines. So, 'why, professing these opinions have I written in verse?', asks Wordsworth (ibid., p. 262). To

which the answer is that linear repetition, far from being integral to poetry, will merely 'superadd' a 'charm' to what is there already, and in any case metre is a source of pleasure, the intention of poetry being to produce pleasure. The argument is inconsistent, and it is only made superficially more consistent by Coleridge in *Biographia Literaria* when the 'mechanical' effect of metre is given a psychological basis as a 'spontaneous effort' at control (1949, II, p. 49).

For Wordsworth in the 'Preface' effectively all previous poetry has been rhetorical. The function of rhetoric, as has been argued, is to *contain* enunciation by holding it into correspondence with the enounced, the sound echoing the sense. In denying the difference between experience and the imitation of experience, the 'Preface' means to *efface* enunciation altogether. Poetry is to be so wholly transparent to experience that it is virtually identical to it.

From Wordsworth's 'Tintern Abbey'

Central to Romanticism is the representation of experiences in which everyday consciousness gives way to a state where subject and object appear a unity; where, in Shelley's words, people 'feel as if their nature were dissolved into the surrounding universe' or as if it were 'absorbed into their being' (1966, p. 174). In Romantic poetry this experience is typically represented in two forms: one starting from the union of subject and object, and moving from it to a distinct ego; another in which the union takes place as a moment during everyday consciousness. In the first form – exemplified by Coleridge's 'Kubla Khan' – a symbolic landscape or situation approximates to a dreamlike state from which a conscious ego emerges, as happens in the last section of 'Kubla Khan' when an 'I' suddenly appears to recall a damsel once seen in a vision. In the second – exemplified by 'Tintern Abbey' – conscious perception is retained and with it awareness of external and internal as separate, though there are moments of a sense of unity, such as that represented in the second paragraph of 'Tintern Abbey' when 'We see into the life of things'. The first paragraph of the poem anticipates this, as the speaker, in describing a landscape, begins to see external nature as a mirror in which his own subjectivity is reflected back.

In 1798 the passage appears as follows (one line being cancelled by the Errata):

Five years have passed; five summers, with the length
Of five long winters! and again I hear
These waters, rolling from their mountain-springs
With a sweet inland murmur.* – Once again
Do I behold these steep and lofty cliffs,
Which on a wild secluded scene impress
Thoughts of more deep seclusion; and connect
The landscape with the quiet of the sky.
The day is come when I again repose
Here, under this dark sycamore, and view
These plots of cottage-ground, these orchard-tufts,
Which, at this season, with their unripe fruits,
Among the woods and copses lose themselves,
Nor, with their green and simple hue, disturb
The wild green landscape. Once again I see
These hedge-rows, hardly hedge-rows, little lines
Of sportive wood run wild; these pastoral farms
Green to the very door; and wreathes of smoke
Sent up, in silence, from among the trees,
With some uncertain notice, as might seem,
Of vagrant dwellers in the houseless woods,
Or of some hermit's cave, where by his fire
The hermit sits alone.

* The river is not affected by the tides a few miles above Tintern. (Footnote original.)

(In the 1845 edition ll. 13–15 are shortened to: 'Are clad in one green hue, and lose themselves / 'Mid groves and copses. Once again I see'.)

Out of the 22 lines (l. 23 is a half-line) in this extract, 14 run on. The blank verse is a condition for strongly varied clause and sentence length, from the four words of the opening ('Five years have passed') to the last sentence, which qualifies 'wreathes of smoke' recursively over four and a half lines. The syntax is built into four confident repetitions: 'again I hear', 'Once again / Do I behold', 'I again repose', 'Once again I see'. The first is in a relatively short sentence, the second two are part of closely parallel sentences, the last is part of one which is complexly subordinated. In an effect anticipated in the Pope passage but taken much further here, syntax is separated from this syntagmatic chain and so freed to work iconically (a point to be taken up later). Donald Davie has affirmed that 'Romantic' syntax is 'phantasmal' since the syntactic forms carry no 'weight of poetic meaning' (1976, p. 63). Here the apparently punctilious subordination in the syntax – for instance in the last sentence – masks an openness in the syntagmatic chain. This moves somewhat arbitrarily from the speaker's memory of five years to the sound of the river, to the cliffs, the sky, then back to himself 'Here', then on again to the farms, the smoke, the gypsies and the hermit. In contrast to the tight linearity of the syntagmatic chain in the description of Belinda, here it has a relatively looser development, weaving between the represented speaker and the landscape he describes. There is some uncertainty about how it gets from one to the other.

Empson showed in 1930 how in the 'philosophic' passage of 'Tintern Abbey' ('And I have felt / A presence . . .') meaning is shuffled across a series of 'grammatical ambiguities' (1961, p. 153). So it is also in the opening paragraph. In the pause at the end of line 6 'impress' seems intransitive (the cliffs impress themselves on the scene) but turns out to be transitive, yielding in addition the semantic surprise that they impress 'Thoughts', an abstract, rather than their own weight, which is concrete. The phrase 'Thoughts of' can be taken either appositionally (thoughts that are secluded) or possessively (thoughts about seclusion). The next verb, 'connect', may have as its subject: (1) the 'I' beholding; (2) the cliffs; (3) the 'Thoughts'. Here the slide is syntactic and syntagmatic. In another example it is only syntagmatic, when the smoke is attributed first to an animate source ('vagrant dwellers') and then without distinction to an inanimate one (the 'hermit's cave').

These slips and disjunctions are marks of enunciation, they imitate the parataxis, the juxtaposed syntax of speech. But they also form part of a consistent slide of signifier over signified. Thus, in the opening paragraph 'wild' refers to natural objects (the 'secluded scene' and 'lines' of wood) but at the end of the poem it means a state of mind (the sister's 'wild eyes' and 'wild ecstasies'). Colin Clarke has pointed out that certain words in the poem, including 'murmur', 'impress', 'quiet', 'deep' and 'lofty', consistently 'refer to external objects and the inner life' (1963, p. 49). Both the concrete and abstract meanings of some words are thematized into a coherent whole, and the slips – such as that over 'connect' – in so far as they produce the *same* ambiguity, are mastered by being rendered semantic. For the passage is *about* the 'peaceful fusion of . . . outer and inner' (Jacobus 1976, p. 110) in a way typical of Romantic poetry, whose common feat is 'to read meanings into the landscape' (Wimsatt 1970, p. 110). The movement between speaker and landscape opens the syntagmatic chain but also helps to close it again. This closure becomes the foundation for the representation of a speaker.

'Tintern Abbey' returns to Renaissance precedents in its use of *discours*, though goes well beyond them in the degree to which the speaker is particularized in space and time. In the opening paragraph the first person singular is used four times. Thick with demonstratives, the passage 'modifies eight nouns in sixteen lines with *this* or *these*' (Woodring 1968, p. 59) and after the initial past tense ('have passed') there follow ten verbs in the present. These are all vivid and insistent marks of enunciation, as is the tendency towards parataxis which, as already noted, gives the impression of speech. The radical use of *discours* is exemplified in the way the description of the hedge-rows is changed halfway through: 'These hedge-rows, hardly hedge-rows, little lines / Of sportive wood run wild'). The interjection ('hardly hedge-rows') and qualification minutely represent the movement of consciousness, the redefining of an object in the very act of describing it. The represented speaker is precisely located in the landscape. When he says

I again repose
Here, under this dark sycamore . . .

the adverb ('Here') deserves the emphasis it takes from its position at the beginning of a line after a run-on ending.

It is not the case that 'In *Tintern Abbey* we discover the poet, sitting – apparently alone – on the banks of the river Wye' (Ferry 1978, p. 107); rather the poem works to situate the reader within the speaker. The effect is like that of a point-of-view shot in the cinema, so called 'subjective camera' in which the audience sees on the screen what a character in the story sees. As Robert Langbaum says, 'we must stand where the poet stands and borrow his eyes' (1963, p. 48) (by 'poet' he means the represented speaker). The referential effect is achieved here not indirectly through irony but directly, for subject and object, speaker and landscape, are posed as reciprocal terms, one as real as the other. The poem, 'by specifically locating the speaker with reference to everything he sees and hears . . . establishes the concreteness . . . of the speaker' (ibid., p. 47). The extensive use of *discours*, 'seeing' through the speaker's eyes, his identity substantiated by direct reference to the represented landscape, these are 'signs of person' which contrive to give the speaker a vivid 'presence'. They go to make up a detailed and plausible script dramatizing the represented speaker and providing the reader with a firm and coherent position as subject of the enounced.

In fact, through a manoeuvre which Robert Young (1979) has examined in 'The Prelude', 'Tintern Abbey' may well represent its speaker as *himself* produced in a process of disjunction between the 'I' of the enounced and the 'I' of enunciation. For example, the speaker identifies himself confidently by saying 'I see / These hedge-rows' but immediately redefines them – and with them himself – by seeing them as something else ('sportive wood'). Of course since this process is portrayed as taking place in the represented speaker, it takes place in what is already the enounced of the poem. The technique gives even greater plausibility to the dramatization of 'presence'. It becomes yet another means by which the reader is invited into identification with the represented speaker.

Romantic poetry works to semanticize enunciation and make it iconic. During the discussion of Shakespeare three kinds of iconicity were distinguished (see above pp. 103–6). In two of them a resemblance was established by means of intonation and in one it was by phonetic means. Traditional iconicity, sound and intonation set up to resemble a phenomenon described, is found throughout Romantic poetry. An example from the passage is 'sportive wood run wild'. After the slow fricatives of 'hedge-rows, hardly hedge-rows', there is a more rapid rhythm on 'sportive wood run wild', which, augmented by the alliteration (wood/wild), the contrast between the vowel /oo/ and diphthong /i/, and the pause after 'wild' leads to 'wild' taking on a drawn out, rising intonation. Once we know the meaning (a wood getting out of human control) then this progression of sound and intonation can be felt to imitate it. Such iconicity, and all the techniques so far examined, only develops further those techniques and effects round which the discourse is founded at the Renaissance. The special innovation of Romantic poetry can be seen in the way it would deal with the process of enunciation. The kind of iconicity by which non-poetic or spoken intonation is represented is taken to an extreme: the poem's enunciation now seeks to conform throughout to the state of mind of its represented speaker. The effect is novel and merits separate designation as *expressiveness*.

The project is no longer to contain the poem's enunciation but to disavow it altogether, exactly according to the programme put forward in the 'Preface' and illustrated there with reference to a Gray sonnet (1965, pp. 252–3). Vocabulary and phrasing associated with poetic discourse are to be avoided in favour of one which imitates non-poetic discourse. For this a necessary condition is normal – that is non-poetic – word-order. And this in turn depends upon rejecting the couplet for blank verse and other lyric metres. Positively, normal word-order helps to dramatize 'presence' through the more plausible imitation of speech; negatively, it steps aside from all the traditional formal rhetoric which demands word-order inversion (as was discussed in relation to Augustan poetry). In the 23 lines which open 'Tintern Abbey' there are only two clear examples of inversion, 'Do I behold' (l. 5) and 'Nor . . . disturb' (l. 14), the second being replaced by normal word-order in 1845. This makes possible a fluent representation of actual, if elevated, speech:

> Five years have passed; five summers, with the length
> Of five long winters! and again I hear
> These waters, rolling from their mountain-springs
> With a sweet inland murmur . . .

Such naturalism is a condition for expressiveness. In these lines the repetition of 'five' three times would be rhetorical if it were not held onto the speaker's represented state of mind: 'The three-fold repetition of "five", combined with the dragging rhythm, creates a felt sense of the weight of time as man experiences it' (Durrant 1969, pp. 34–5). Similarly the word 'again' is repeated four times in the passage but made expressive of the speaker's nostalgic pleasure in finding perception confirms memory.

The effect has been noted under various names by conventional criticism, and only one other example is needed here. Geoffrey Hartman argues that 'in the opening verses of "Tintern Abbey" . . . there is a *wave effect* of rhythm whose characteristic is that while there is internal acceleration, the feeling of climax is avoided' (1964, p. 26). After detailing this, he claims that the 'rhythm . . . is linked in "Tintern Abbey" to a vacillating calculus of gain and loss, of hope and doubt' (ibid., p. 27). I find this account convincing, and would only add that the place where the 'vacillating calculus' occurs is the mind of the represented speaker. Thus a complex movement of the poem's enunciation, one involving syntax, intonation and metre, is held in close relation to the enounced by being rendered expressive.

Expressiveness is pervasive in a way iconicity is not. Limits are always set on iconicity because it relies on a perception of similarity – between Belinda and linguistic features in the poem, for example. There is no such limit to expressiveness since it aims to subsume the poem altogether. The poem's process of enunciation itself is to be identified with the enunciation of the represented speaker. No aspect of enunciation is to be excluded from this effect, which would completely identify the reader's production of the poem with the represented speaker. The difference between traditional iconicity and Romantic expressiveness can be related to that between realism and naturalism. A realist theatre imitates everyday reality but is consciously played 'to' the audience by actors very much aware of its existence (e.g. Congreve's *The Way of the World*). Naturalist theatre would deny the existence of the audience altogether and treat the proscenium arch as a transparent 'fourth wall' through which the uninvited audience peeps. As Ibsen said in 1874, 'it was the illusion of reality I wanted to produce' (1970, p. 82). The technique is anticipated in Romantic poetry in its attempt to efface the process of enunciation and come across as though it were experience itself, just as in Wordsworth's programme the poetry *is* the powerful feeling.

Coventional criticism thus reads 'Tintern Abbey' in terms of the 'presence' it represents, seeing the poem as

> supported throughout by a further insistent stress on the power of affection, infused not merely into the repetitive use of particular words but into the tender conversational tone, the gentle, even rhythm, and the patient unfolding of the argument, all working expressively to reveal the persona of a poet who has learned to devote himself to the affections of the heart and who invites the reader, by participating in the same processes, to share what he has discovered. (Beer 1978, p. 74)

Thus, 'the poem emerges as something more than a set of ingenious rhetorical devices' (ibid.). But a poem can never be more than rhetoric and device, whether clumsy or ingenious, since it can never be other than a poem. It can only create 'presence', reveal 'the persona of a poet', as the effect of poetic techniques, closure in the syntagmatic chain, the use of *discours*, the referential effect, forms of iconicity and expressiveness. The tradition that in the poem 'Wordsworth speaks' weighs so heavily it may help to refer the issue to another medium for clarification. Mainstream cinema constantly works to suggest that actors and actresses are really present in a film. As John O. Thompson has shown in a brilliant and witty essay on film acting, the feeling of a star's ineffable presence is brought about by various definite and analysable semiological features (1978, pp. 55–69). And the face itself is produced by light shining through transparent celluloid onto a flat screen. The presence of the star is an effect of the means of representation, and so is that of 'Wordsworth' in 'Tintern Abbey'. A poem can only be a Poet by being a poem first.

My vocabulary – 'contrives', 'works', 'represents', 'imitates', 'dramatize', 'script' – is meant to exhibit the poem as a process of enunciation. 'Tintern Abbey' gives the effect of the presence of a speaker by denying its presence as a poem. It offers a position for the reader as the subject of the enounced, a position which, disavowing the enunciation producing it, is thus self-present and autonomous. Romantic poetry, in continuing to privilege the transcendental ego, rejoins and sustains the inherited poetic discourse rather than challenging it. In fact in aiming to efface rather than contain enunciation, it would fix this position even more decisively. Finally symptomatic of this is the way Romanticism modifies traditional prosody rather than breaking with it. A programme intending to imitate 'the real language of men' should tend logically to free verse. Though it unseats the Augustan couplet and introduces a variety of lyric metres, Romantic poetry re-affirms the dominance of the bourgeois metre, iambic pentameter, and exploits it for traditional purposes. For an alternative to the dominant discourse one has to turn back to the ballad or forward to Modernism, to Ezra Pound and free verse.

9

The Modernism of Eliot and Pound

to dissolve the hard cement of an
apparently impregnable fortress: syntax

Tristan Tzara,
Le Surréalisme au Service de la Révolution

Eliot and tradition

Modernism, defined as the modernism of Eliot and especially Pound, comprehensively challenges the English poetic tradition, even if it does not succeed in overthrowing it. The whole field of the inherited discourse is subverted in one way or another. The coherence of the syntagmatic chain is disrupted by various fissures, dislocations and *lacunae*, and opened up to forms of parataxis. Closed and repetitive verse forms are generally abandoned. Iambic pentameter is violently rejected in favour of 'free verse' – as 'Canto 81' says, 'to break the pentameter, that was the first heave.' Although there is of course no question of a return to the feudal ballad, modern poetry and especially that of the 'Cantos' is more like the ballad than it is like anything from the intervening discourse of the bourgeois epoch. At stake in modernism, once again, is the definition of subject position. All the tactics, including those given manifesto treatment as 'the tradition' and the 'ideogram', can be understood as working towards a single end – to foreground signifier over signified, to acknowledge that the reader is positioned as subject of enunciation producing the enounced of the poem. Modernist poetry can be seen as denying a position for the transcendental ego. By insisting on itself as production it asserts the subject as made, constituted, relative rather than absolute. The view is explicit in both Pound and Eliot.

Asked in 1930 about his beliefs Pound replied:

> Given the material means I would replace the statue of Venus on the cliffs of Terracina. I would erect a temple to Artemis in Park Lane. (1973, p. 53)

The post-Christian belief that 'God is dead' supposes his continued presence as a god-shaped hole: in Pound's paganism the absolute God of Christianity is simply not in question. Nor is the notion of the subject as unified, absolute, transcendental:

> In the 'search for oneself', in the search for 'sincere self-expression', one gropes, one finds some seeming verity. One says 'I am' this, that or the other, and with the words scarcely uttered one ceases to be that thing. (Pound 1960, p. 85)

This anticipates precisely the Lacanian distinction between subjects of the enounced and of enunciation: the 'I' spoken about in the enounced ('"I am" this, that or the other') is always sliding away from the speaking subject ('one says') across the process of enunciation. This is also the founding position of Eliot's essay, 'Tradition and the Individual Talent':

> The point of view which I am struggling to attack is perhaps related to the metaphysical theory of the substantial unity of the soul. (1966, p. 19)

The essay assumes that the subject, far from being a transcendental unity, is decentred both in being an effect of discourse and in being structured through a dynamic of conscious and unconscious. The second topic has been discussed in detail by C. K. Stead, who concludes that when he wrote the essay Eliot was 'obsessively concerned . . . with a process of poetry in which the conscious will played only the minor role of sub-editor' (1967, p. 131).

'Tradition and the Individual Talent' is effectively a point-by-point refutation of Wordsworth's 'Preface' (which it cites). The case is as follows:

1 Poetic tradition is affirmed as a point of origin for poetry

rather than the poet as an author, a personality. In tradition 'the existing monuments form an ideal order among themselves'. Thus, poetry is recognized as an autonomous discourse with a specific mode of enunciation. This is exactly that aspect of poetry Wordsworth objected to – and hoped to overcome – because it was 'mechanical'. The poet is an effect of this discourse and not its source; he is 'only a medium and not a personality' (1966, p. 20).

2 While the 'Preface' was concerned to deny if possible the difference between poetry and prose, between literature and life, Eliot's essay insists that 'the difference between art and the event is always absolute' (ibid., p. 19). The difference is that in poetry the role of language – of signification – is dominant.

3 This is brought out in the deliberate distinction between 'emotions' and 'feelings'. 'Emotions' or 'actual emotions' belong to personality and to life, but 'feelings' are specific to poetry because language is integral to them – 'feelings' inhere 'in particular words or phrases or images' (ibid., p. 18). 'Emotions' appertain to 'the man who suffers', the world of event, but 'feelings' belong to art, to 'the mind which creates', as does 'the poet's mind' in 'seizing and storing up numberless feelings, phrases, images'. Whatever may be the case for language in general (after the remark about 'the unity of the soul' the essay halts at this frontier) in poetry signifier stands prior to signified and words create experience rather than experience being 'communicated' through words.

An important role is accorded to the signifier in Eliot's theory of the 'objective correlative':

> The only way of expressing emotion in the form of art is by finding an 'objective correlative'; in other words, a set of objects, a situation, a chain of events which shall be the formula of that *particular* emotion . . . (ibid., p. 145)

In Wordsworth's conception emotion can be directly expressed in art ('poetry is . . .'). Eliot's account denies that emotion can be directly expressed: art is at best 'correlative' to emotion, and then only because the emotion can be represented by a 'formula', a 'set of objects'. In poetry these objects are signifiers, thus acknowledged as having a weight and materiality of their own which makes the transparent expression of emotion or experience impossible. My summary may make Eliot's position more coherent than it actually is. The essays of 1919 are contradictory. They want to break with the Romantic inheritance but don't have a theory of language that will let them.

The activity of the signifier in Eliot's poetry can be seen most clearly in the undermining of a consistent feature in the traditional discourse, the referential effect. 'Morning at the Window' is a poem from the 1917 volume:

> They are rattling breakfast plates in basement kitchens,
> And along the trampled edges of the street
> I am aware of the damp souls of housemaids
> Sprouting despondently at area gates.
>
> The brown waves of fog toss up to me
> Twisted faces from the bottom of the street,
> And tear from a passer-by with muddy skirts
> An aimless smile that hovers in the air
> And vanishes along the level of the roofs.

On one side the speaker's words describe external reality: from an upper window he hears the activity of housemaids in basements and looks down at the crowd on the pavement; their white faces stand out against the fog which distorts them, one smiles up at him before vanishing. On the other, the words take on meaning in terms of subjective fantasy: from the bottom of a brown sea waves toss up dead bodies with twisted faces, sometimes in their violence tearing the face from the skull. Although object and subject can be forced into place, in the poem description keeps collapsing into fantasy: the housemaid's soul is a damp weed and the passer-by's smile (like the Cheshire cat or the Magritte painting of the huge red mouth) hovers at roof level. These are surrealist images which suggest – as in the passage from F. H. Bradley cited approvingly in the note to line 411 of 'The Waste Land' – that 'My external sensations are no less private to my self than are my thoughts or my feelings'. 'Morning at the Window' is evidence that language can no longer be treated as a transparent medium through which the represented speaker knows a supposedly external reality. Subject and object are no longer represented as reciprocally held in place, and the referential effect is not achieved.

Yet the poem still represents a speaker, an 'I' aware of itself and its feelings, even if these cannot be confidently assigned between external sensation and internal thought. 'The Waste Land' does not represent a coherent speaker posed firmly between external and internal. But it can be read as someone's stream of consciousness, a psychological continuity held onto a centre, however scattered. Even if I'm falling apart I'm still an 'I' – the dispersed ego continues to be an ego. The gaps and disruptions of the text thus become the *expression* of a disintegrating mind, one sinking progressively into hallucination and finally delirium (the last eleven lines). 'Objective correlative' may in fact be a precise description. Signifiers are given the licence to 'float' in their own autonomy but only so they can be correlative to an incoherent state of mind. In Pound the effect is always more radical. An apt contrast to 'Morning at the Window' is 'In a Station of the Metro':

> The apparition of these faces in the crowd;
> Petals on a wet, black bough.

Three phrases, the title being one, are juxtaposed without verbs. They are not unified as expressions of a state of mind and the reader is led to consider how these faces in the crowd are like – and unlike – petals on a bough, not to identify with a speaker represented as seeing things that way. With this poem Pound is well on his way to the theory of the ideogram. Though idiosyncratic, this outlines a programme for a complete break with the inherited poetic discourse.

Pound and the ideogram

For Pound – as also for Brecht and Eisenstein – oriental culture is attractive because it promises a way out from under the centredness and 'soul-obsession' of Western art. 'In a Station of the Metro' imitates a Japanese *haiku*, and Pound describes it as a 'one-image poem', defining this as 'a form of superposition, that is to say, it is one idea set on top of another' (1960, p. 89). The conception of juxtaposition rather than subordination can be explained with reference to Fenollosa's essay on 'The Chinese Written Character as a Medium for Poetry', which Pound edited and published in 1920.

Saussure says there are only two systems of writing, phonetic and ideographic. The writing system of Modern English is phonetic because it 'tries to reproduce the succession of sounds that make up a word'. In an ideographic system the written sign or character is not related to the sound but 'stands for a whole word and, consequently, for the idea expressed by the word', and the 'classic example' of this 'is Chinese' (1959, p. 26). Because of this ideographic feature Fenollosa argues that Chinese characters are 'based upon a vivid shorthand picture of the operations of nature' (1962, p. 140). For example, in

the ideograms are pictures:

> First stands the man on his two legs. Second, his eye moves through space: a bold figure represented by running legs under an eye, a modified picture of an eye, a modified picture of running legs . . . Third stands the horse on his four legs. (ibid.)

Chinese writing 'speaks at once with the vividness of painting, and with the mobility of sounds'. In reading it 'we do not seem to be juggling mental counters, but to be watching *things* work out their own fate' (ibid.).

Fenollosa's view asserts that Chinese writing is, in Peirce's terms, iconic rather than symbolic (see above, p. 103). This may be contested, however. According to Richard Newnham 'the rationale of Chinese writing has at least five separate elements' and though the origin of its characters 3000 years ago may have been pictorial 'about nine-tenths of modern Chinese characters' depend upon a phonetic element (1971, pp. 34 and 38). This can be illustrated from Fenollosa's own example, for none of these characters could be recognized as pictures or cartoons of a man, an eye or a horse unless one knew already what they represented (though Pound claims Gaudier-Brzeska could do it). So the ideogram is at least as much phonetic as it is iconic, and so remains subject to Saussure's principle that 'the bond between the signifier and the signified is arbitrary' (1959, p. 67). In any case, even as visual rather than verbal signifier the ideogram produces signifieds and not things in themselves such as 'the operations of nature'. Failure to distinguish clearly between signified and referent, the object it may refer to, has led to serious confusion in some accounts of the ideogram (Alan Durant's being a scrupulous exception, 1981). Kenner's view that 'the poet connects, arranges, defines *things*' (1951, p. 77) does not even have Fenollosa's own cautious and necessary qualification that with the ideogram we 'seem' to be watching things. And Donald Davie has praised the description of the ant in 'Canto 83' because 'the ant is outside the human mind' (1965, p. 177). Ants of course are independent of the human mind but the concept or signified 'ant' in 'Canto 83' remains indelibly inside language and so inside the human mind, for, as Davie has correctly pointed out elsewhere, 'every word *is* an idea' (1976, p. 138). Reference is another matter altogether, and there is no question in poetic discourse of 'watching *things*'.

Misconceptions about the nature of the ideogram have obscured what is surely its main significance as a model for poetry. The written character of Chinese is a radical demonstration that a means of representation is integral to thought. It evidences precisely the 'mechanical' feature of discourse and writing which Derrida defines as the 'graphematic'. It is not the supposedly iconic feature of Chinese writing that makes it an important model for poetry. Rather it is the way that the writing, in virtue of being ideographic rather than phonetic, foregrounds and insists upon the materiality of the signifier. In Derrida's account this is the 'irreducibly graphic poetics' of Fenollosa and Pound, which threatens to decentre the subject by exhibiting its dependency on language (1976, p. 92). In the ideogram the things we watch working out their own fate are words.

Further at issue over the ideogram and Fenollosa's essay is not simply Chinese *writing* but the model of discourse provided by the Chinese *language*. When he comments on Fenollosa in *ABC of Reading* Pound emphasizes the method of the language, how it builds up an abstract concept from particulars. To get a general idea – red – it puts together

> the abbreviated pictures of
>
> | ROSE | CHERRY |
> |---|---|
> | IRON RUST | FLAMINGO |
>
> That, you see, is very much the kind of thing a biologist does (in a very much more complicated way) when he gets together a few hundred or a thousand slides, and picks out what is necessary for his general statement. Something that fits the case, that applies in all of the cases. (1961, p. 22)

This summary has also led to confusion, one compounded by the historical author who elsewhere makes the often-cited assertion that 'An idea is only an imperfect induction from fact' (1963, p. 267). This pragmatist viewpoint, preferring facts to ideas, retains the empiricist opposition between facts and ideas, experiment and theory. The opposition cannot be sustained. Scientific hypotheses are not simply general statements derived from facts by induction; it is 'only theory that could constitute them as facts in the first place' (Stedman Jones 1972, p. 113). The biologist's slides take on significance within the theory and practice of biology and the criteria established there for what counts as a fact (see Hirst 1979, pp. 18–21).

This is not said in order to refute Pound's views, and poetry does not stand or fall with the epistemology of its historical author. It is meant to clear the ground so as to direct attention to the model of the ideogram as an alternative to rhetoric, abstraction and what Pound calls 'emotional slither'. Pound's version of the Renaissance, the Quattrocento discovery of 'personality', lays blame on rhetoric and, crucially, syntagmatic coherence:

> And in the midst of these awakenings Italy went to rot, destroyed by rhetoric, destroyed by the periodic sentence and by the flowing paragraph . . . (1960, p. 113)

The 'periodic sentence': this is where the 'search for oneself' may seem to find completion in an 'I am' this, just as in the Lacanian conception of subjectivity the ego discovers itself in the coherence of the syntagmatic chain. But in the method of the ideogram 'syntax yields to parataxis' (Hesse 1969, pp. 47–8). So much is clear from Fenollosa:

> For example, the ideograph meaning 'to speak' is a mouth with two words and a flame coming out of it. . . . In this process of compounding, two things added together do not produce a third thing but suggest some fundamental relation between them. (1962, p. 141)

The method sets signs alongside each other rather than subordinating them in the syntagmatic chain to produce 'a third thing'. This is hardly surprising since 'the Chinese language naturally knows no grammar' (ibid., p. 145):

> 'Reading promotes writing' would be expressed in Chinese by three full verbs. Such a form is the equivalent of three expanded clauses and can be drawn out into adjectival, participial, infinitive, relative or conditional members. One of many possible examples is, 'If one reads it teaches him how to write'. Another is, 'One who reads becomes one who writes'. But in the first condensed form a Chinese would write, 'Read promote write'. (ibid., p. 152)

Strict coherence in the syntagmatic chain provides a position for the transcendental ego. Such is the place offered in and by the precise, explicit and completed syntax of Fenollosa's examples. The Chinese language suggests a radical alternative to this procedure and the subject position it offers.

The parataxis of Chinese opens a possible way out from syntagmatic closure by giving something else instead. Somewhat mysteriously this is defined by Pound as 'the image', that which is at 'the furthest possible remove from rhetoric' (1960, p. 83). Through its use

> The artist, working in words only, may cast on the reader's mind a more vivid image . . . he works not with planes or with colours but with the names of objects and of properties . . . to cast a more definite image than the layman can cast. (ibid, p. 121)

Although 'working in words only' the image promises to combine something of the two-dimensional simultaneity of graphic representation with the temporal linearity inherent in language. Poetry following this principle would have 'one idea set on top of another' (ibid., p. 89) even while the discourse moved forward along the syntagmatic chain.

I think Pound's term *image* implies a use of words more characteristic of thing-presentations than word-presentations (in Freud's terminology). While conscious expression takes the form mainly of word-presentations (verbal signifiers), the unconscious 'thinks' only in thing-presentations (visual signifiers: see 'The Unconscious', Freud 1957, XIV, p. 201). Here is where the iconic properties of the ideogram may come in. It is because the discourse of the unconscious 'speaks' in thing-presentations that the dream-thought seeks representation in images:

> the dream-work makes a translation of the dream-thoughts into a primitive mode of expression similar to picture-writing. All such primitive systems of expression, however, are characterized by indefiniteness and ambiguity. . . . (Freud 1973, p. 267)

The 'picture-writing' of dreams is ambiguous for two related reasons. The 'syntax' of dreams is necessarily paratactic: 'dreams are unable to represent logical relations' because they are imagistic and so 'reproduce *logical connection* by *simultaneity in time*' (Freud 1977, pp. 423–4). And images or pictures are inherently polysemous. This is especially the case in dream images, for these exhibit *condensation*, that is, they are the outcome of a 'superimposing' of 'separate elements' or meanings which Freud compares to 'what happens if you take several photographs on the same plate' (1973, p. 206). To try to grasp this polysemy Freud turned to languages which use ideographic script, including Chinese, in the hope of finding analogies for 'the indefiniteness of dreams' (ibid., p. 269). He was not disappointed. Like dreams, Chinese 'has practically no grammar' and 'any expression of relations is omitted'; nevertheless Chinese made sense, as in the following proverb:

> 'Little what see much what wonderful'. This is not hard to understand. It may mean: 'The less someone has seen, the more he finds to wonder at'; or: 'There is much to wonder at for him who has seen little'. (ibid., pp. 269–70)

The translations attempt to close the syntagmatic chain in exactly the same way as they do when Fenollosa translates the condensed form 'Read promote write'. Freud goes on to point out that languages make sense while a dream 'does not want to say anything to anyone'.

The 'Cantos' are not dreams. As language – word-presentations – they are necessarily committed to significance in a temporal dimension and so to syntagmatic relations. In the ideogram units are added together, rose, cherry, iron rust, flamingo: in the verbal equivalent the precise delimitation of the unit is not clear – whether word, phrase, sentence, or narrated event – but it is clear that the basis is *unitary*, as in the ballad. So William Carlos Williams recognized in an early review:

> the word has been used in its plain sense to represent a thing – remaining thus loose in its context – not gummy – (when at its best) – an objective unit in the design . . . and discreet (= discrete). (Sullivan 1970, pp. 121–2)

In the syntagmatic chain the units are not glued together but proceed paratactically and so 'with the addition of each new component the trajectory changes direction' (Kenner 1951, p. 63). Each unit is vividly conceived, pictorial and so likely to be multivalent. Accordingly, the individual ideogram has a place in the main chain developed horizontally; at the same time, down the vertical axis, it works in many-tracked association with (potentially) all the others, 'read back and forth in the light of each other' (Cook 1969, p. 359). The syntagmatic chain does not try to close upon itself but rather to stay open to meanings that slide in relation to each other 'underneath' it. The reading progresses from unit to unit, each forming associations with others, but never reaching an absolute centre, a final term.

From Pound's 'Canto 84'

In the 'Cantos' vocabulary, speech register, kind of discourse, and national language shift from unit to unit and line to line. Chinese characters, Greek script, musical scores, italics, capitals all jostle together. Continuous linear indentation bears the mark of the typewriter's shift key, as does the frequent use of parenthesis and abbreviation, even including the use of special typewriter keys, @ and %. Opening 'Canto 84' the reader is confronted with a typeface which insists that it is graphematic, an instance of *writing*:

8th October:
Si tuit li dolh el plor
Angold τέθνηκε
tuit lo pro, tuit lo bes
Angold τέθνηκε
'an' doan you think he chop an' change all the time
stubborn az a mule, sah, stubborn as a MULE,
got th' eastern idea about money'
Thus Senator Bankhead
'am sure I don't know what a man like you
would find to *do* here'
said Senator Borah
Thus the solons, in Washington,
on the executive, and on the country, a.d. 1939
ye spotted lambe
that is both blacke and white
is yeven to us for the eyes' delight
and now Richardson, Roy Richardson,
says he is different
will I mention his name?
and Demattia is checking out.
White, Fazzio, Bedell, *benedicti*
Sarnone, two Washingtons (dark) J and M
Bassier, Starcher, H. Crowder and
no soldier he although his name is Slaughter
this day October the whateverth Mr Coxie
aged 91 has mentioned bonds and their
interest
apparently as a basis of issue
and Mr Sinc Lewis has not
and Bartók has left us
and Mr Beard in his admirable condensation
(Mr Chas. Beard) has given one line to the currency
at about page 426 'The Republic'
We will be about as popular as Mr John Adams
and less widely perused
and the he leopard lay on his back playing with straw
in sheer boredom,
(Memoirs of the Roman zoo)

in sheer boredom
Incense to Apollo
Carrara
snow on the marble

snow-white
against stone-white
on the mountain
and as who passed the gorges between sheer cliffs
as it might be by, is it the Garonne?
where one walks into Spagna
that Ho-Kien heard the old Dynasty's music
as it might be at the Peach-blossom Fountain
where are smooth lawns with the clear stream
between them, silver, dividing,

and at Ho Ci'u destroyed the whole town
for hiding a woman, Κύθηρα δεινά

and as Carson the desert rat said
'when we came out we had
80 thousand dollar's worth'
('of experience')
that was from mining
having spent their capital on equipment
but not cal'lated the time for return
and my old great aunt did likewise
with that too large hotel
but at least she saw damn all Europe
and rode on that mule in Tangiers
and in general had a run for her money

like Natalie

'perhaps more than was in it'

Under white clouds, cielo di Pisa
out of all this beauty something must come.

(This is the Faber text 1954, pp. 572–4. All page numbers are taken from this edition. A slightly different text is given in Pound's reading of the poem on the record, *Caedmon* TC 1122.)

Except when the word is treated solely as a thing – as in certain Dada and concrete poems – there is always a syntagmatic chain, however slight. In these lines syntax is used locally in units, these being divided off by *lacunae* between lines as well as by indentations isolating parts of lines and even single words. There is nevertheless a consecutive syntagmatic chain, a dominant meaning, in which the text is to be read as a discourse of political economy. ('Canto 84' is marked historically as a product of what Thomas Pynchon's novel *Gravity's Rainbow* names as 'the Zone', Europe 1944–45.)

> Today, in 1945, true currency and virtue have passed away, along with millions of war dead. Bad leadership (Roosevelt the mule) and the deficit finance introduced by the New Deal have led to the slaughter and suffering of war, to soldiers put into prison camps (list of names). Today Jacob Coxey has repeated his concern about finance capital, a concern ignored by Sinclair Lewis and given insufficient attention by Charles Beard. One might die of boredom. Yet the earth remains beautiful in the mountains north of Pisa and the passes of the Pyrenees, though this counts for little unless the leaders remember to exercise virtue instead of arbitrary power ('destroyed the whole town'). Individual experience, like that of Kit Carson, can still triumph over mere wealth. The sky remains beautiful. . . .

There is syntagmatic coherence, more clearly perhaps in this concluding Canto of the 'Pisan' section than in others, but the coherence is provisional and opens onto a field of associated connotations and meanings, as will be discussed later. The enounced of 'Canto 84' is not closed and does not strive to give a fixed and absolute position for the reader as subject of the enounced.

In default of a coherent enounced, 'Canto 81' does not set up a consistent narrator or represented speaker. Symptomatic of this is the way the extract refuses any decisive commitment to *discours* or *histoire*. As in the ballad, the transitions between *discours* and *histoire* are rapid and unannounced, even more so in Pound's performance than on the page. The first 'I' is Senator Bankhead, a character in the enounced, and the 'you' he addresses (l. 6) is the American writer and polemicist, Ezra Pound, who immediately reappears as the narrator, the 'I' of 'will I mention his name?' The first person 'us' (l. 17) is used impersonally for mankind but the 'us' whom Bartók has left means our generation. The 'We' of line 35 is indefinite – possibly the American people, possibly our generation again, possibly a group of economic polemicists which includes Ezra Pound. The next slide is especially interesting. The person listing those in the camp now appears in the third person *within* the enounced, Ezra Pound the 'he leopard' lying on his back (l. 37). Can the 'same' person be at the disposal of both *discours* and *histoire*? If 'Ezra Pound' is represented as speaking who is this other 'Ezra Pound' being spoken about? The effect is comparable to the momentary dislocation that occurs when Alfred Hitchcock catches a bus in the action of an Alfred Hitchcock film. But here the disruptive effect is not momentary but chronic. Instead of the traditional manoeuvre to disavow enunciation by establishing a firmly coherent enounced with either a consistently represented speaker (*discours*) or narrator (*histoire*), there is an open and pleasurable exchange between *discours* and *histoire*. The reader's position as subject of the enunciation is not denied while the reader is forced to identify with a represented speaker, the supposed 'I' of 'Shakespeare' or 'Wordsworth'. Rather the shifting 'I' of 'Canto 84' becomes available as a position in the text for the reader producing the text in the present: the 'I' of 'will I mention his name?' is opened for occupation by the reader who is actually doing the mentioning.

No attempted closure in the syntagmatic chain, no consistent use of *discours/histoire*, no speaker coherently represented and so no referential effect substantiating this dramatization – expectations descending from the traditional discourse weigh on our reading of Modernist poetry and make it hard to describe in positive terms. 'Canto 84' offers pleasure – the pleasure of the joke, both release from the inhibition imposed by the 'serious use of words' (Freud 1976, p. 168) and pleasure in the active play of associations that the signifier produces once freed from strict duty in the syntagmatic chain. Saussure diagrams the way chains of association depend on each word down the paradigmatic axis. From each ideogram – often each word – in the 'Cantos', 'tentacular roots' reach down to form seemingly infinite reticulations of meaning with others depending on other ideograms. There is room here to consider only a few illustrations, beginning with *mule* and *white* in the extract.

In the main horizontal chain of meaning the repeated 'mule'

(l. 7) is a metaphor describing Roosevelt. Even within these 71 lines it recurs, in line 66 ('mule in Tangiers'), the context prescribed for it in the syntagmatic chain being quite different. Possibly these two meanings can be thematized, as was the slide of meanings 'night'/'(k)night' in 'Sonnet 73', the 'silver' of the Thames in 'The Rape of the Lock', or between 'external' and 'internal' connotations of a set of words in 'Tintern Abbey'. Possibly the recalcitrance of Roosevelt is 'answered' by the great aunt's domination of her mule. But the Tangier 'mule' is also hashish (perhaps picking up the 'Tangier' reference from 'Canto 74', p. 459), and in any case the 'mule' has a place in a menagerie of animals in this canto: 'lambe' (l. 15), 'leopard' (l. 37), 'rat' (l. 56) (there are also pigs – 'suini' – in the part I've not quoted). These meanings are not led back into coherence in the main syntagmatic chain, but form a minor chain of their own carried in suspension 'beneath' the major chain. Another example is *white*, which takes on contrasted meanings in 'white' lamb, 'White' as a man's name (l. 22), 'snow-white' and 'stone-white' (ll. 44–5), 'white' clouds (l. 70). And does 'snow-white' also connote the heroine of the fairy-tale filmed by Walt Disney in 1937?

These examples are from one passage in one canto. They are hugely multiplied if we bring in others, even keeping just to the 'Pisan Cantos'. The 'he leopard' (l. 37) rejoins the 'leopard' by its water dish (p. 458), the attendant 'leopards' (p. 464), the lynx of the 'Lynx Song' (beginning p. 520), the Plantagenet 'leopards' mourned in 'Canto 80' (p. 550) as well as the lizard with 'leopard spots' (p. 551) and the 'caged panther' (p. 565). A concordance might show something of this but it would not reveal that the leopard, sacred to Dionysos, connotes male vitality so that these contexts are linked with others. The 'Cantos' do not suppose that desire can be contained in monogamy – rather they assert that for a man there should be 'Tre donne' (p. 514), three women either as lovers or the feminine in three roles as wife, lover, daughter. The theme surfaces often in the main syntagmatic chain, but even when it does not it is sustained at other levels in the polysemy. In the extract Κύθηρα δεινά (terrible Cytherean Aphrodite, l. 55), 'mountain' (l. 46), 'clouds' (l. 71) and 'eyes' (l. 17) each pick up strands of association (in emphasizing the 'lyric mode' of the 'Cantos' Eugene Nassar has already outlined something of this effect, see

1975). For example, the figure of *Aphrodite* as she was when born from the sea at Cythera in Greece (and so painted as 'La Nascita' by Botticelli) constantly recurs (in the 'Pisan Cantos' on pp. 457, 461, 472, 474, 485, 488, 498, 521, 523, 525, 534, 545, 546, 552, 555, 560), as do *mountain*, *clouds*, *eyes*. But these parallel strands (to keep the metaphor) resonate in harmony with others they are linked to. To cite only some main instances: Aphrodite and mountain in 'Mt Taishan/femina, femina' (p. 457) (Taishan is the poem's name for a mountain behind Pisa); Aphrodite and cloud in 'the veil of faint cloud before her/ Κύθηρα δεινὰ (p. 546); Aphrodite and eyes in 'her eyes as in "La Nascita"' (p. 474); cloud and mountain in 'Mist covers the breasts of Tellus-Helena' (p. 503) (two other mountains near Pisa are likened to women's breasts); mountain and eyes in 'green of the mountain pool/shone from the unmasked eyes' (p. 556); cloud, eyes, and mountain in 'eyes are like the clouds over Taishan' (p. 565).

Pleasurable in itself, this erotization of landscape becomes more so through the mode of its representation: with the loosening of the main syntagmatic chain, substitutions that would otherwise be excluded 'down' the paradigmatic axis are activated and 'unconsciously call to mind a host of other words' (Saussure 1959, p. 123) along and across the 'Cantos'. In comparing poetry to music Lacan says:

> one has only to listen to poetry . . . for a polyphony to be heard, for it to become clear that all discourse is aligned along the several staves of a score. There is in effect no signifying chain that does not have, as if attached to the punctuation of each of its units, a whole articulation of relevant contexts suspended 'vertically', as it were, from that point. (1977a, p. 154)

The description applies to all discourse but especially to poetry. Yet bourgeois poetic discourse acts to suppress this polysemy. The extent to which Pound's poetry breaks with the inherited tradition can be seen in the way Lacan's description applies to 'Canto 84' and the operation in it of the units *Aphrodite*, *mountain*, *clouds*, *eyes*.

Since closure is not attempted in the syntagmatic chain there is no coherent enounced. Since there is no such enounced, enunciation cannot be subordinated to it and held onto it – consequently there cannot be traditional iconicity in 'Canto 84'. Instead, pervading every phrase there is a flexible and extraordinarily varied *coincidence* between enunciation and enounced. A repeated slowing and falling intonation marks out a trajectory with the same shape as that of the meaning in

> playing with straw
> in sheer boredom,
> (Memoirs of the Roman zoo)
> in sheer boredom.

And in 'out of all this beauty something must come' the intonation rising onto the last word corresponds to the idea of some good emerging (Pound's performance makes 'come' an imperative and the line speaks both of the beauty of the natural world and – self-reflexively – of the beauty of the poem).

From the start of the bourgeois tradition the attempt was to subordinate signifier to signified, enunciation to enounced, a subordination which was noted particularly in the area where the phonetic properties of language most threatened to manifest themselves, that is when two words were linked by sound in a rhyme. Rhyme does not have to be treated this way. In the ballad, it was argued, there is a coincidence between sound and meaning in the verse-form and rhyme. Relative to subordination, the effect is to foreground enunciation, and that is precisely the effect also in 'Canto 84'. There is no regular verse form so there is no rhyme, but the 'rhyme effect' is achieved. The play of the signifier in which words are treated as things is as it were displaced all over the enunciation. One indication of this is the open activity of the signifier in the form of homonyms in the extract. The tendentious or 'adult' play on words is sardonically parodied with the play on 'interest' and 'issue' (ll. 28–9) while the 'childish' jest, in which one signifier governs two unrelated signifieds, is welcomed. All the names show this. A door is a jar when it's ajar, and similarly J. P. Angold, killed in 1943, is also 'and gold'. Senator 'Bankhead' sounds like a bank head, 'Borah' a borer, and 'Slaughter' like a soldier even if he is not a fierce one. 'Sinc Lewis' is a sink, and no doubt Charles 'Beard' is a beard just as 'Coxie' is cocksy. Words here are being treated as things as well as words.

Another instance of the same feature, one particularly apparent in Pound's recorded performance, is the way the text invites an insistent and emphatic pronunciation. This is appropriate because, negatively, there is no iambic pentameter with its abstract pattern to even out peaks and troughs of syllable prominence, and, positively, because the ever-present coincidence of enunciation and enounced intensifies stress and promotes syllable prominence. The result, especially in Pound's reading aloud, is comparable to the chanting called for by the old four-stress metre, though it is achieved by wholly different means. It leads to the singable quality mentioned often by Pound, that 'Poetry must be read as music' (1963, p. 437).

Lacking strict closure in the syntagmatic chain 'Canto 84' provides a position for the subject contrasting entirely with that offered in the texts previously analysed as typifying developments in bourgeois poetic discourse. Instead of a position for the transcendental ego, 'Canto 84' works to give a place for the subject as *relative*, not absolute. The openness of the syntagmatic chain to paradigmatic substitutions acknowledges dependence of the ego on the discourse which produces it. At the same time in according precedence to the signifier the text accepts the speaking subject as effect rather than origin of discourse – as made up 'in there' among the words rather than coming to them from somewhere outside. The reader is not to identify with the apparent self-sufficiency of a represented speaker but, on the contrary, to be positioned in a field of forces, a moving point in the process of enunciation and subjectivity. Here as always the text works for but cannot compel the reader to take up a subject position, and most conventional criticism still reads Pound's poetry as though it were Wordsworth's ('Pound says', etc). Nevertheless, as Maud Ellman argues in an excellent short essay, the 'Cantos' introduce a discourse which 'corrodes, at every moment, the empire of the cogito' (1979, p. 18), the empire, that is, of the Cartesian ego, for which being is equated with self-consciousness.

A necessary condition for this effect is the use of 'free verse'. Pound believes in 'absolute rhythm', a rhythm that 'corresponds exactly to the emotion or shade of emotion to be expressed' (1963, p. 9). This exact correspondence cannot take place when the abstract pattern of pentameter is imposed throughout and when closure of the syntagmatic chain tries to run everything together. It can only happen when the poetry is divided into units with each unit finding a local rhythm and intonation, this in turn leading to that coincidence between enunciation and enounced which foregrounds the signifier. The question of 'free verse' relates back to the account of pentameter in Chapter 4 and is a topic in itself.

Intonational metre

In 1893 Gustave Kahn advocated the 'ingeniously varied touches (*effleurements*)' of free verse in place of the 'symmetry of the metronome' demanded by traditional metres (1912, p. 35). Similarly Pound, in 1912, by his own account, decided to 'compose in the sequence of the musical phrase, not in sequence of a metronome' (1963, p. 3). I believe that this envisages a metric based on repetition and difference in intonation contour. The term *free verse*, as Graham Hough has shown (1960, pp. 90–4), covers much that is merely loose iambic pentameter, as well as a genuinely new form. And the term is merely negative, describing what the new form lacks in relation to the old, as in Eliot's 1917 essay 'Reflections on "Vers Libre"', which defines 'free verse' as '(1) absence of pattern, (2) absence of rhyme, (3) absence of metre' (1953, p. 88). A name which recognizes the positive features of the new metric is *intonational metre* and I shall use that.

The definition of intonation is not easy and remains still partly controversial. Intonation is determined phonetically, syntactically, and semantically, a product of three factors in which the intonation contours of a language are also themselves a fourth determinant. Intonation can only be defined for speech, not writing, since writing can always be spoken aloud in different ways. It is the spoken feature that distinguishes between 'What shall we have for dinner, mother?' and 'What shall we have for dinner . . . mother?' Among the available and, unfortunately, competing descriptions of English intonation are Trager and Smith (1951), O'Connor and Arnold (1961), Halliday (1967), Crystal (1969). Selected by Bolinger (1972) to discuss the intonation system of English, Crystal is the most authoritative. He describes intonation in terms of tone-units:

> In English there seem to be regular definable phonological boundaries for tone-units in normal (here meaning mainly 'not too hurried') speech. Given that each tone-unit will have one peak of prominence in the form of a nuclear pitch movement . . . , then it is the case that after this nuclear tone there will be a tone-unit boundary which is indicated by two phonetic factors. (1969, p. 205)

These two factors are a change of pitch and a juncture of some kind, usually a slight pause. Tone-units are *not* the same as sentences or clauses, though they can coincide. The obligatory element of a tone-unit is a word carrying a glide, a sustention in its accentual syllable, and this is referred to as the nucleus. A unit can consist of one word, as in Beckett's *Endgame*, when Nell responds to Nagg's complaint that there is now sand on the bottom of his ashbin:

> *Nagg*: It was sawdust once.
> *Nell*: Once!

As well as a nucleus a tone-unit can have a head, 'the stretch of utterance extending from the first stressed and usually pitch-prominent syllable (or onset) up to, but not including, the nuclear tone'; it consists of 'an unspecified number of stressed and unstressed syllables' (ibid., p. 207). There can also be a prehead, syllables with varying lesser degrees of stress before the head; similarly, others after the head form a nuclear tail:

> A tone-unit accordingly may be internally defined as a structure consisting of one of the following: P(rehead), H(ead), N(ucleus), T(ail) . . . summarizable as (P) (H) N (T), where brackets include optional elements. (ibid., p. 208)

Intonation is a spoken effect and so 'generally, the faster the speech the longer the tone-units (measured in terms of words)' (ibid., p. 256). Even though punctuation and typography may help, it isn't easy to illustrate a tone-unit on the page. In a statement 'So once upon a time there were three *bears*' (i.e. not rabbits), 'So' is the prehead, 'once' the onset for the head, this stretching to the nuclear tone, which is a falling one on '*bears*' (having ten syllables the utterance would serve in context as a line of iambic pentameter). With the meaning changed to 'So once upon a time there were *three* bears' (i.e. not four) '*three*' is sustained to become the nuclear tone while 'bears' is now a tail. Other contours are possible, for example if the utterance is divided into two tone-units with sustention giving a nuclear tone at 'time': 'Once upon a *time* . . . there were three *bears*'.

Crystal classifies the permutations and combinations possible in intonation contour. The prehead may have four possible areas of pitch-height, the head may be either falling or rising or falling-rising (-falling) or rising-falling (-rising). Classification of possible nuclear tones begins with the distinction between simple, compound and complex; tails generally continue the direction (rise or fall) of the nuclear tone or begin this way and level out. A more complete summary is not needed for this present account: what matters is Crystal's assertion that there is 'tonal reduplication' or 'cohesion', that 'tone-units do not exist in isolation, but work in sequences in connected speech' (ibid., p. 235). The implication is clear. The tendency of intonation contours to recur means that intonation can be used in a poem to make up a pattern of repetition from which there can be significant variation. Consequently intonation can provide the basis of a metre, a principle for line organization through 'parallelism of the signifier'.

We have seen that it was the contribution of the Russian Formalists to specify the *dominanta* or defining feature of poetry as line organization (see Chapter 4). In doing so they challenged traditional accounts of line organization in terms of the abstract pattern of a metre and defined the line as rhythm and intonation: 'Our theory of verse was founded on the analysis of rhythm as the structural basis of verse' (Eichenbaum 1965, p. 124). This approach to poetry is still relatively disregarded in the Anglo-American tradition, but recently Crystal, pursuing his work on intonation, has come up with fresh evidence of its validity. The essay 'Intonation and metrical theory' gives the results of an analysis of intonation contour produced when a number of different readers read aloud from four poetic texts. Two of these were traditional iambic pentameter (part of Gray's 'Elegy' and the Wordsworth sonnet 'Composed upon Westminster Bridge'), and two (from Eliot's 'Prufrock' and 'The Dry Salvages') were loose iambic pentameter (see Hough 1960, pp.

90–4). Crystal found that all the lines in the samples could be defined in terms of intonation: 'All lines were coterminous with tone-unit boundaries, with the sole exception of cases that would traditionally be called "enjambement" . . . 80 per cent of all lines consisted of a single tone-unit' (1975, pp. 119–20).

The conclusion should not be surprising. The abstract pattern of pentameter requires discourse to be divided into lines of ten syllables. This in itself is enough to ensure that most lines will be tone-units, as Traugott and Pratt point out: 'verse lines commonly form syntactic units ending with a normal pause (comma or sentence break), and thus tend to conform to the intonation system of normal speech' (1980, p. 74). So, as Crystal shows, lines of iambic pentameter will exhibit repetition and parallelism of the signifier in their intonation *quite apart* from the requirement of the abstract pattern that unstressed and stressed syllables should alternate. And if traditional accentual-syllabic metres *already* work partly on the basis of intonation repetition it is reasonable to suppose there can be intonational metre which operates only on this basis. In 1935 Jakobson claimed that in 'free' verse 'intonation becomes the dominant' (1971a, p. 82), a view he reaffirmed many years later in stating that there are varieties of 'so-called vers libre that are based on conjugate intonations and pauses only' (1960, p. 360). The Formalist approach to line organization was taken further in the Prague School, notably by Mukařovský. From an anlysis of examples of 'free verse' in French, Czech and German, he concluded that each exhibited a common principle of organization, 'a special intonation, characterized above all by a strongly marked melodic formula, at the end of each line' so that 'the rhythmic outline is given only by this intonation' (1933, p. 155). This again suggests that repetition in the intonation contour is sufficient basis of unity in a poem to mark variations and difference. It remains to be shown that this is Pound's programme.

Eliot affirms that poetry should work with a contrast between 'fixity and flux', doubts whether 'free verse' can provide enough fixity, and so advocates loose blank verse on the model of Webster and Middleton (1953, p. 89). Similarly Yvor Winters has attacked Pound's metrical practice because it fails to lay down a 'substructure insisting steadily on the identity of the poem' (1960, p. 145). In the face of such comments it is very clear that Pound accepts the principle that poetry should exhibit repetition and difference, for he affirms that 'Art is a departure from fixed positions; felicitous departure from a norm' (Sullivan 1970, p. 73). It would take a long and detailed study by someone proficient in the linguistics of intonation to demonstrate that intonational repetition does establish a basis of unity in each of the poems. What I shall argue here is that this is indeed the tendency of Pound's own theoretical statements.

ABC of Reading gives an explicit and accurate account of the relation between stress and intonation:

> In making a line of verse (and thence building the lines into passages) you have certain primal elements:
>
> That is to say, you have the various 'articulate sounds' of the language, of its alphabet, that is, and the various groups of letters in syllables.
>
> These syllables have differing weights and durations
>
> A original weights and durations
>
> B weights and durations that seem naturally imposed on them by the other syllable groups around them.
>
> Those are the medium wherewith the poet cuts his design in TIME. (1961, pp. 198–9).

As was explained above (see pp. 55–8), there is a stress inhering in the isolated word and there is also syllable prominence as produced by the word's context in the intonation contour. Not only do the syllables 'build into' lines on the basis of intonation but – crucially – *lines can build into sections and whole poems on the same basis*. This is the clear implication of the early essays gathered together as 'A Retrospect'. Pound believes in 'absolute rhythm', one which 'corresponds exactly to the emotion or shade of emotion to be expressed' (1963, p. 9). To get this correspondence different topics will need very different rhythms. So some 'vers libre' has an accent as 'heavily marked as a drum-beat' (ibid., p. 12), while some may use rhythms that, though appropriate to the theme, are too 'tenuous and imperceptible'. Heavily marked rhythms obviously have a clear principle of repetition but others, even while corresponding to the topic, are insufficiently repetitive to be firmly perceived.

The poem needs this perceptible recurrence, and so the use of 'vers libre' is justified 'only when the "thing" builds up a rhythm more beautiful than that of set metres, or more real, more a part of the emotion of the "thing", more germane, intimate, interpretative than the measure of regular accentual verse; a rhythm which discontents one with set iambic or set anapaestic' (ibid., p. 12). This rhythm that *builds up* from line to line must be working with 'tonal reduplication' (in Crystal's term), that is, a degree of repetition in the intonation able to take over the function of a traditional metre such as pentameter.

Elsewhere Pound even anticipates one obvious problem in trying to define intonation – that it is a feature of speech, not writing:

> All typographic disposition, placings of words *on* the page, is intended to facilitate the reader's intonation, whether he be reading silently to self or aloud to friends. Given time and technique I might even put down the musical notation of passages or 'breaks into song'. (Sullivan 1970, p. 192)

Once again intonation is referred to the singable feature of language. This was written in 1939. There has been no need to try to write down the intonation contours for those poems available on records in Pound's version of the spoken performance. Possibly the tone-units and contours of that performance should be regarded as part of the 'canonical' text of the poem.

In default of the abstract pattern of traditional metre much discussion of intonational metre has been able to discern in it no principle of repetition at all. In searching for repetition as a fixed mastery which 'continueth throughout the verse' it has failed to perceive that a poem may develop from one kind of repetition at the beginning to quite another at the end. Iambic pentameter works to disclaim enunciation and to offer a point 'outside' or abstracted from the specificities of the poem, a centre round which every detail and line can cohere and so one that 'blurs them together', as Donald Davie found in Pound's 'Provincia Deserta'. For these reasons, as was argued earlier, the traditional metre of English poetry helps to provide a position for the reader as transcendental ego. Intonational metre exhibits the possibility of a completely different kind of poetry. The tendency of this metre is to insist on enunciation and to render the poem as – in Pound's words – a 'design in TIME', a continuously variable development in which meaning, intonation and the line organization of the poem are relative to each other; a development, therefore, which is never fixed onto an absolute centre. In these respects intonational metre acts to provide a *relative* position for the reader, one shown to be produced in the process of enunciation.

10

A future for poetry

The poetry of a people takes its
life from the people's speech and
in turn gives life to it.

Eliot,
The Use of Poetry and the Use of Criticism

Despite the contrast in their historical position, as the previous chapter suggested, there are a number of similarities between the ballad and 'The Cantos'. There is one huge difference. It can be indicated by means of the linguistic distinction between sociolect and idiolect, between (roughly) language as related to a social group, however defined, and language as related to one person. The ballad is a sociolect in that any single text combines units of event, motif, and phrasing from other ballads, so drawing on a common and intersubjective discourse. 'The Cantos' are an idiolect, in that most of their allusions and references are to the intellectual and personal biography of one man, though given currency by constant repetition in the poem. This was understood by Pound to the extent that he regarded 'a modern Eleusis' as being 'possible in the wilds of a man's mind only' (1952, p. 294). In this respect 'The Cantos' remain deeply individual and at present accessible only to a tiny elite of readers.

Lucien Goldmann writes that 'The most important consequence of the development of a market economy is that the individual . . . now becomes . . . an independent element, a sort of monad, a *point of departure*' (1973, p. 18). In underwriting this view the present study has sought to analyse bourgeois poetic discourse as producing, according to the specificities of poetry, a position for the supposedly unified 'individual' as 'point of departure' for discourse rather than its effect. The term 'bourgeois' describes such a discourse as characterizing not just a period but an epoch of history. But if this epoch is over – or if not over, at least since 1848 in its terminal crisis – what happens to the poetic discourse appropriate to it? It can hardly be denied that the canonical tradition, the poetry of the 'single voice', is now dying both from inward exhaustion and external erosion. Since the work of the great Modernists sixty years ago – work whose project anyway was to subvert the inherited discourse – where has that tradition shown unmistakable signs of its continuing vitality? Charles Olson, for example, asserts that poetry can only move forward 'by getting rid of the lyrical interference of the individual as ego, of the "subject" and his soul' (1960, p. 395), a principle which dismisses all the tradition stands for. Bourgeois poetic discourse now has no real audience. It is kept alive only in a tainted and complicit form. The state promotes it in secondary and higher education as part of the syllabus for public examinations and 'English' degrees. In Britain the state also subsidizes such poetry through the Arts Council, which gives money for readings and magazines. Meanwhile, people are much more interested in such genuinely contemporary media as cinema, television and popular song in its many varieties.

In terms of contemporary poetry across the world, the scope comprehended by Ruth Finnegan's *Oral Poetry*, or even in the context of the history of European culture, a poetic discourse specially intended for performance by the individual speaking voice is exceptional. Most poetry in most epochs has been linked intimately with music and dancing, and so with a range of social institutions. Subsequent to a separation between dance and song, bourgeois poetic discourse was founded in a further separation of poetry from music, as John Stevens describes. Since the realistic representation of a voice speaking is inscribed into its enunciation it is designed to be spoken by an individual, a good actor who – in our earlier example – can perform the poem as a script dramatizing the 'presence' of Shakespeare speaking 'nakedly as "I"'. Pound should be taken literally when he says that 'Poetry atrophies when it gets too far from music' (1961, p. 61). There seems no reason to believe that the canonical tradition will continue and no particular reason to regret that it's had its day. There seem good grounds to suppose that poetic discourse will live on, especially if it is reunited with music and even with dancing as well.

This present study has tried to describe English poetry as a discourse defined in the way it foregrounds and promotes a position for the reader as subject of the enounced while aiming to disavow the reader's position as subject of enunciation. Typically this effect has been sought by the consistent representation of a speaker by all the means at the disposal of poetic discourse. The study has aimed itself to be a discourse of knowledge, one to be judged for its accuracy in the analysis of its object. But it has also operated what might be called a 'socialism of the text'; that is, in asking the reader to work through linguistic details that give the text its effect it has aimed to expropriate the poem from its supposed 'owner', the represented speaker or narrator, and put it back into the hands of the reader who produces it.

To confront the dominant discourse as a whole from the Renaissance down to Modernism it has been necessary to try to advance on all fronts at once. Inevitably this strategy has meant resources have been overstretched and that some salients remain weakly established and inadequately defended. Rhyme, irony and the referential effect, iconicity, expressiveness – for discussion of each of these matters existing concepts have been taken over and adapted so as to enable the main argument to move forward. Each deserves separate treatment. The relation between syntax and the syntagmatic chain, and the related question of polysemy and thematized meanings, need further consideration. There has been no illustration of the repetition and difference made possible by intonational metre. The question whether the dominant discourse is typically a 'masculine' rather than 'feminine' form has not even been asked, and an answer remains to be found, possibly along lines suggested by Julia Kristeva (1974). This study has meant to establish a problematic for the analysis of poetic discourse and to illustrate its scope and explanatory potential by developing it in detail, so exposing topics for further analysis. In so doing, it has accepted that no text is ever closed, none is ever more than provisional, including this one now ending.

Texts

'Three Ravens' 1611, *The English and Scottish Popular Ballads*, ed. F. J. Child, 5 vols, vol. 1 (Child 26 A) (New York: Cooper Square Publishers, 1965).

'Sonnet 73', William Shakespeare, 1609, *Shakespeare's Sonnets, Facsimile of the First Edition* (London: Oxford University Press, 1905).

'The Rape of the Lock', Alexander Pope, 1714, *The Poems of Alexander Pope*, ed. John Butt (London: Methuen, 1965).

'Tintern Abbey', William Wordsworth, 1798, *Lyrical Ballads 1798* (Merston, Yorkshire: The Scolar Press, 1971).

'Morning at the Window', T. S. Eliot, 1917, *Collected Poems 1909–1962* (London: Faber, 1966).

'In a Station of the Metro', Ezra Pound, 1916, *Collected Shorter Poems* (London: Faber, 1968).

'Canto 84', Ezra Pound, 1949, *The Cantos of Ezra Pound* (London: Faber, 1954).

All texts are reproduced as they appeared in their first English book publication.

References

Althusser, Louis, 1977, *Lenin and Philosophy and Other Essays*, tr. Ben Brewster (London: New Left Books).

Attridge, Derek, 1981, 'The language of poetry: materiality and meaning', *Essays in Criticism*, vol. 31, no. 3, 228–45.

——1982, *The Rhythms of English Poetry* (London: Longman).

Bacon, Francis, 1951, *The Advancement of Learning* (London: Oxford University Press).

Barrett, Michèle and Radford, Jean, 1979, 'Modernism in the 1930s: Dorothy Richardson and Virginia Woolf', in Francis Barker *et al.* (eds), *1936: The Sociology of Literature,* 2 vols (Colchester: University of Essex).

Barthes, Roland, 1972, *Mythologies*, tr. Annette Lavers (London: Cape).

——1975, *S/Z*, tr. Richard Miller (London: Cape).

——1976, *The Pleasure of the Text*, tr. Richard Miller (London: Cape).

——1977, *Image-Music-Text*, tr. Stephen Heath (London: Fontana).

Beckett, Samuel, 1958, *The Unnameable*, tr. by the author (New York: Grove Press).

Beer, John, 1978, *Wordsworth and the Human Heart* (London: Macmillan).

Belsey, Catherine, 1980, *Critical Practice* (London: Methuen).

Bennett, Tony, 1979, *Formalism and Marxism* (London: Methuen).

Benveniste, Emile, 1971, *Problems in General Linguistics* (Miami: University of Miami Press).

—— 1974, *Problèms de Linguistique Générale*, vol. 2 (Paris: Gallimard).

Bold, Alan, 1979, *The Ballad* (London: Methuen).

Bolinger, Dwight L., 1965, 'Pitch accent and sentence rhythm', in Isamu Abe and Tetsuya Kanekiyo (eds), *Forms of English, Accent, Morpheme, Order* (Cambridge, Mass.: Harvard University Press).

—— (ed.), 1972, *Intonation, Selected Readings* (Harmondsworth: Penguin).

Boomsliter, Paul C., Creel, Warren and Hastings, George S., 1973, 'Perception and English poetic metre', *PMLA*, 88, 200–8.

Booth, Stephen, 1969, *An Essay on Shakespeare's Sonnets* (New Haven: Yale University Press).

Booth, Wayne C., 1961, *The Rhetoric of Fiction* (Chicago: University of Chicago Press).

Brecht, Bertolt, 1964, *Brecht on Theatre*, ed. and tr. John Willett (London: Eyre Methuen).

Buchan, David, 1972, *The Ballad and the Folk* (London: Routledge & Kegan Paul).

Caudwell, Christopher, 1946, *Illusion and Reality, A Study of the Sources of Poetry* (London: Lawrence & Wishart).

Chapman, Raymond, 1973, *Linguistics and Literature* (London: Edward Arnold).

Chatman, Seymour, 1965, *A Theory of Metre* (The Hague: Mouton).

—— and Levin, S. R. (eds), 1967, *Essays on the Language of Literature* (Boston: Houghton Mifflin).

—— (ed.), 1971, *Literary Style: A Symposium* (London: Oxford University Press).

Clarke, Colin, 1963, *Romantic Paradox* (London: Routledge & Kegan Paul).

Cohen, Murray, 1977, *Sensible Words, Linguistic Practice in England 1640–1785* (Baltimore and London: Johns Hopkins University Press).

Cole, A. Thomas, 1972. 'Classical Greek and Latin', in W. K. Wimsatt Jr (ed.), *Versification, Major Language Types* (New York: New York University Press).

Coleridge, Samuel Taylor, 1917, *Poems*, ed. E. H. Coleridge (London: Oxford University Press).

——1949, *Biographia Literaria*, ed. J. Shawcross, 2 vols (London: Oxford University Press).

Collier, Andrew, 1979, 'In defence of epistemology', in John Mepham and D. H. Ruden (eds), *Issues in Marxist Philosophy*, 3 vols (Brighton: Harvester).

Cook, Albert, 1969, 'Rhythm and person in "The Cantos"', in Eva Hesse (ed.), *New Approaches to Ezra Pound* (London: Faber).

Coulthard, Malcolm, 1977, *An Introduction to Discourse Analysis* (London: Longman).

Crystal, David, 1969, *Prosodic Systems and Intonation in English* (Cambridge: Cambridge University Press).

——1975, *The English Tone of Voice* (London: Edward Arnold).

Davie, Donald, 1965, *Ezra Pound, Poet as Sculptor* (London: Routledge & Kegan Paul).

——1976, *Articulate Energy, An Inquiry into the Syntax of English Poetry* (London: Routledge & Kegan Paul).

Derrida, Jacques, 1976, *Of Grammatology*, tr. Gayatri Chakravorty Spivak (Baltimore and London: Johns Hopkins University Press).

——1977, 'Signature event context', *Glyph*, 1, 172–97.

Dryden, John, 1962, The Poems and Fables, ed. James Kinsley (London: Oxford University Press).

——1967/68, *Of Dramatic Poesy and other Critical Essays*, ed. George Watson, 2 vols (London: Dent).

Durant, Alan, 1981, *Ezra Pound, Identity in Crisis* (Brighton: Harvester).

Durrant, Geoffrey, 1969, *William Wordsworth* (London: Cambridge University Press).

Eagleton, Terry, 1976, *Criticism and Ideology* (London: New Left Books).

Easthope, Antony, 1981, 'Towards the autonomous subject in poetry: Milton "On His Blindness"', in Francis Barker *et al.* (eds), *1642: Literature and Power in the Seventeenth Century* (Colchester: University of Essex).

Eichenbaum, Boris, 1965, 'The theory of the "Formal Method"', in Lee T. Lemon and Marion J. Reis (eds), *Russian Formalist Criticism: Four Essays* (Lincoln: University of Nebraska Press).

Eliot, T. S., 1953, 'Reflections on "Vers Libre"' (1917), in John Hayward (ed.), *Selected Prose* (Harmondsworth: Penguin).

——1957, *On Poetry and Poets* (London: Faber).

——1966, 'Tradition and the individual talent', *Selected Essays* (London: Faber).

——1970, *The Use of Poetry and the Use of Criticism* (London: Faber).

Ellman, Maud, 1979, 'Floating the Pound: the circulation of the subject of "The Cantos"', *Oxford Literary Review*, 3(3), 16–27.

Empson, William, 1961, *Seven Types of Ambiguity* (Harmondsworth: Penguin).

Epstein, E. L., 1978, *Language and Style* (London: Methuen).

—— and Hawkes, Terence, 1959, *Linguistics and English* (Buffalo: Buffalo University Press).

Fenollosa, Ernest, 1962, 'The Chinese written character as a medium for poetry', in Karl Shapiro (ed.), *Prose Keys to Modern Poetry* (New York: Harper & Row).

Ferry, David, 1978, *The Limits of Mortality: An Essay on Wordsworth's Major Poems* (Westport, Connecticut: Greenwood).

Finnegan, Ruth, 1977, *Oral Poetry* (Cambridge: Cambridge University Press).

Fish, Stanley E., 1974, *Self-Consuming Artifacts: the Experience of Seventeenth-Century Literature* (Berkeley: University of California Press).

Forrest-Thomson, Veronica, 1978, *Poetic Artifice* (Manchester: Manchester University Press).

Foucault, Michel, 1970, *The Order of Things* (London: Tavistock).

Fowler, Roger, 1966, 'Prose rhythm and metre', in Roger Fowler (ed.), *Essays on Style and Language* (London: Routledge & Kegan Paul).

——1971, *The Languages of Literature* (London: Routledge & Kegan Paul).

——1975, *Style and Structure in Literature* (Oxford: Basil Blackwell).

Francis, Nelson, 1965, *The English Language* (New York: Norton).

Freeman, D. C. (ed), 1970, *Linguistics and Literary Style* (New York: Holt, Rinehart & Winston).

Freud, Sigmund, 1957, 'The unconscious' (1915), *Standard Edition*, tr. James Strachey, XIV (London: Hogarth Press).

——1973, *Introductory Lectures on Psychoanalysis*, tr. James Strachey (Harmondsworth: Penguin).

——1976, *Jokes and Their Relation to the Unconscious*, tr. James Strachey (Harmondsworth: Penguin).

——1977, *The Interpretation of Dreams*, tr. James Strachey (Harmondsworth: Penguin).

Frye, Northrop, 1957, *Anatomy of Criticism* (Princeton: Princeton University Press).

Gardner, Helen, (ed.) 1965, *John Donne: 'The Elegies' and 'The Songs and Sonets'* (London: Oxford University Press).

Gerould, G. H., 1932, *The Ballad of Tradition* (Oxford: Clarendon Press).

Goldmann, Lucien, 1973, *The Philosophy of the Enlightenment*, tr. Henry Maas (London: Routledge & Kegan Paul).

Graves, Robert and Riding, Laura, 1925, *Contemporary Techniques of Poetry, A Political Analogy*, Hogarth Essays no. 8 (London: L. & V. Woolf).

Group Mu, 1977, *Rhétorique de la Poésie* (Brussels: Éditions Complexe).

Halle, Morris and Keyser, S. R., 1966, 'Chaucer and the study of prosody', in D. C. Freeman (ed.), *Linguistics and Literary Style* (New York: Holt, Rinehart & Winston).

——1971, *English Stress* (New York: Harper & Row).

Halliday, M. A. K., 1967, *Intonation and Grammar in British English* (The Hague: Mouton).

Halpern, Martin, 1962, 'On the two chief metrical modes in English', *PMLA*, 77(3), 177–86.

Hammond, Gerald, 1981, *The Reader and Shakespeare's Young Man Sonnets* (London: Macmillan).

Hartman, Geoffrey, 1964, *Wordsworth's Poetry 1787–1814* (New Haven: Yale University Press).

Hawkes, Terence, 1973, *Shakespeare's Talking Animals* (London: Edward Arnold).
Heath, Stephen, 1974, 'Lessons from Brecht', *Screen*, 15(2), 103–28.
——1977, 'Language, literature, materialism', *Sub-Stance*, 17, 67–74.
——1981, 'Narrative space', *Questions of Cinema* (London: Macmillan).
——and Skirrow, Gillian, 1977, 'Television: a world in action', *Screen*, 18(2), 7–57.
Hendricks, William O., 1976, *Grammars of Style and Styles of Grammar* (Amsterdam, New York and Oxford: North-Holland).
Hesse, Eva, 1969, 'Introduction', in Eva Hesse (ed.), *New Approaches to Ezra Pound* (London: Faber).
Hirst, Paul, 1979, *Law and Ideology* (London: Macmillan).
Hobbes, Thomas, 1908, 'Preface to Homer', in J. E. Spingarn (ed.), *Critical Essays of the Seventeenth Century*, 3 vols (Oxford: Clarendon Press).
Hough, Graham, 1960, *Image and Experience, Studies in a Literary Revolution* (London: Duckworth).
——1970, 'Criticism as a humanist discipline', in Malcolm Bradbury and David Palmer (eds), *Contemporary Criticism* (London: Edward Arnold).
Ibsen, Henrik, 1970, *Henrik Ibsen, A Critical Anthology*, ed. James McFarlane (Harmondsworth: Penguin).
Jacobus, Mary, 1976, *Tradition and Experiment in Wordsworth's 'Lyrical Ballads'* (London: Oxford University Press).
Jakobson, Roman, 1960, 'Concluding statement: linguistics and poetics', in T. A. Sebeok (ed.), *Style in Language* (Cambridge, Mass.: MIT Press).
——1965, 'Quest for the essence of language', *Diogenes*, 51, 21–37.
——1971a, 'The dominant' (1935), in L. Matejka and K. Pomorska (eds), *Readings in Russian Poetics* (Cambridge, Mass.: MIT Press).
——1971b, 'Shifters, verbal categories, and the Russian verb' (1957), *Word and Language* (The Hague and Paris: Mouton).
——and Halle, Morris, 1956, *Fundamentals of Language* (The Hague: Mouton).
Jones, John A., 1969, *Pope's Couplet Art* (Athens, Ohio: Ohio University Press).
Kahn, Gustave, 1912, 'Le vers libre' (1893), *Premiers Poèmes*, 3rd edn (Paris: Eugene Figuière).
Kenner, Hugh, 1951, *The Poetry of Ezra Pound* (London: Faber).
——1980, 'Pope's reasonable rhymes', in Maynard Mack and James A. Winn (eds), *Pope: Recent Essays* (Brighton: Harvester).
Kenyon Review symposium, 1956, Essays by Harold Whitehall, Seymour Chatman, Arnold Stein, John Crowe Ransom, *Kenyon Review*, 18(3), 411–77.

Kiparsky, Paul, 1977, 'The rhythmic structure of English verse', *Linguistic Inquiry*, 8(2), 189–247.

Knight, G. Wilson, 1955, *The Mutual Flame, On Shakespeare's Sonnets* (London: Methuen).

Knights, L. C., 1964, 'Shakespeare's Sonnets', *Explorations* (Harmondsworth: Penguin).

Kristeva, Julia, 1974, *La Révolution du Langage Poétique* (Paris: Éditions du Seuil).

Lacan, Jacques, 1972, 'Of structure as an inmixing of otherness prerequisite to any subject whatever', in Richard Macksey and Eugenio Donato (eds), *The Structuralist Controversy* (Baltimore and London: Johns Hopkins University Press).

——1977a, *Écrits*, tr. Alan Sheridan (London: Tavistock).

——1977b, *The Four Fundamental Concepts of Psychoanalysis*, tr. Alan Sheridan (London: Hogarth Press).

Land, Stephen K., 1974, *From Signs to Propositions: The Concept of Form in Eighteenth-Century Semantic Theory* (London: Longman).

Langbaum, Robert, 1963, *The Poetry of Experience, The Dramatic Monologue in Modern Literary Tradition* (New York: Norton).

Lanham, Richard, 1976, *The Motives of Eloquence, Literary Rhetoric in the Renaissance* (New Haven: Yale University Press).

Leavis, F. R., 1967, *Revaluation* (Harmondsworth: Penguin).

——1972, *New Bearings in English Poetry* (Harmondsworth: Penguin).

Leech, G. N., 1969, *A Linguistic Guide to English Poetry* (London: Longman).

Leishman, J. B., 1968, *Themes and Variations in Shakespeare's Sonnets* (London: Hutchinson).

Lewis, C. S., 1954, *English Literature in the Sixteenth Century* (London: Oxford University Press).

Lord, Albert B., 1960, *The Singer of Tales* (Cambridge, Mass.: Harvard University Press).

MacCabe, Colin, 1976, 'Theory and film: principles of realism and pleasure', *Screen*, 17(3), 7–27.

——1978, *James Joyce and the Revolution of the Word* (London: Macmillan).

—— 1981, 'On discourse', in Colin MacCabe (ed.), *The Talking Cure* (London: Macmillan).

Machiavelli, N., 1975, *The Prince*, tr. George Bull (Harmondsworth: Penguin).

MacNeice, Louis, 1938, *Modern Poetry* (Oxford: Oxford University Press).

Magnuson, Karl and Ryder, Frank G., 1970, 'The study of English prosody: an alternative proposal', *College English*, 31, 789–820.

——1971, 'Second thoughts on English prosody', *College English*, 33, 198–216.

Marx, Karl, 1970, *Capital*, vol. 1 (London: Lawrence & Wishart).

——1973, *Grundrisse*, tr. Martin Nicolaus (Harmondsworth: Penguin).

——and Engels, F., 1950, *Selected Works*, 2 vols (London: Lawrence & Wishart).

——1970, *The German Ideology*, ed. C. J. Arthur (London: Lawrence & Wishart).

McLuhan, Marshall, 1962, *The Gutenburg Galaxy* (London: Routledge & Kegan Paul).

Metz, Christian, 1975, 'The imaginary signifier', tr. Ben Brewster, *Screen*, 16(2), 14–76.

Mukařovský, Jan, 1933, 'Intonation comme facteur de rythme poétique', *Archives Néerlandaises de Phonétique Experimentale*, 8–9, 153–65.

——1964. 'Standard language and poetic language', in Paul L. Garvin (ed.), *A Prague School Reader* (Washington DC: Georgetown University Press), 17–30; and 'The connection between prosodic line and word order in Czech verse', ibid., 113–32.

Nassar, Eugene Paul, 1975, *The Cantos of Ezra Pound, The Lyric Mode* (Baltimore and London: Johns Hopkins University Press).

Newnham, Richard, 1971, *About Chinese* (Harmondsworth: Penguin).

Nowell-Smith, Geoffrey, 1976, 'A note on history/discourse', *Edinburgh Magazine 1976*, 26–32.

Nowottny, Winifred, 1965, *The Language Poets Use* (London: Athlone Press).

O'Connor, J. D. and Arnold, G. F., 1961, *Intonation of Colloquial English* (London: Longman).

Olson, Charles, 1960, 'Projective verse', in Donald M. Allen (ed.), *The New American Poetry* (New York: Grove Press).

Ong, Walter J., 1982, *Orality and Literacy* (London: Methuen).

Opie, Iona and Peter, 1951, *The Oxford Dictionary of Nursery Rhymes* (Oxford: Clarendon Press).

——1967, *The Lore and Language of Schoolchildren* (London: Oxford).

Oxford Classical Dictionary, 1970, ed. N. G. L. Hammond and H. H. Scullard, 2nd edn (London: Oxford University Press).

Pope, Alexander, 1956, *The Correspondence of Alexander Pope*, ed. George Sherburn, 5 vols (London: Oxford University Press).

Pound, Ezra, 1952, *Guide to Kulchur* (London: Peter Owen).

——1960, *Gaudier-Brzeska, A Memoir* (1916) (Hessle, Yorkshire: Marvell Press).

——1961, *ABC of Reading* (London: Faber).

—— 1963, *Literary Essays of Ezra Pound*, ed. T. S. Eliot (London: Faber).

—— 1973, *Selected Prose 1909–1965*, ed. William Cookson (London: Faber).

Puttenham, George, 1968, *The Arte of English Poesie* (1589) (Merston, Yorkshire: The Scolar Press).

Roubaud, Jacques, 1978, *La vieillesse d'Alexandre: Essai sur quelques états récents du vers français* (Paris: Maspero).

Saintsbury, George, 1910, *A History of English Prosody*, 3 vols (London: Macmillan).

Saussure, Ferdinand de, 1959, *Course in General Linguistics*, tr. Wade Baskin (New York: Philosophical Library).

Shapiro, Karl and Beum, Robert, 1965, *A Prosody Handbook* (New York: Harper & Row).

Shelley, P. B., 1966, *Shelley's Prose, or the Trumpet of a Prophecy*, ed. D. L. Clark (Albuquerque: University of New Mexico Press).

Sidney, Philip, 1947, 'An Apology for Poetry', in Edmund D. Jones (ed.), *English Critical Essays* (*Sixteenth, Seventeenth and Eighteenth Centuries*) (London: Oxford University Press).

Smith, Barbara Herrnstein, 1968, *Poetic Closure: A Study of How Poems End* (Chicago: University of Chicago Press).

Sprat, Thomas, 1908, 'The history of the Royal Society' (1667), in J. E. Spingarn (ed.), *Critical Essays of the Seventeenth Century*, 3 vols (Oxford: Clarendon Press).

Stead, C. K., 1967, *The New Poetic: Yeats to Eliot* (Harmondsworth: Penguin).

Stedman Jones, Gareth, 1972, 'History: the poverty of empiricism', in Robin Blackburn (ed.), *Ideology in Social Science* (London: Fontana).

Stevens, John, 1979, *Music and Poetry in the Early Tudor Court* (Cambridge: Cambridge University Press).

Sullivan, J. P. (ed), 1970, *Ezra Pound, Penguin Critical Anthologies* (Harmondsworth: Penguin).

Thompson, John, 1961, *The Founding of English Metre* (London: Routledge & Kegan Paul).

Thompson, John O., 1978, 'Screen acting and the commutation test', *Screen*, 19(2), 55–69.

Tillotson, Geoffrey, 1962, *On the Poetry of Pope*, 2nd edn (Oxford: Clarendon Press).

Tillyard, E. M. W., 1929, *The Poetry of Sir Thomas Wyatt* (London: Scholartis Press).

Todorov, Tzvetan, 1981, 'Enunciation', in Oswald Ducrot and Tzvetan Todorov (eds), *Encyclopedic Dictionary of the Sciences of Language*, tr. Catherine Porter (Oxford: Basil Blackwell).

Tomashevsky, Boris, 1965, 'Sur le vers', *Théorie de la Littérature, Texts des Formalistes Russes reunies*, ed. and tr. Tzvetan Todorov (Paris: Éditions du Seuil).

Trager, G. L. and Smith, H. L., 1951, *An Outline of English Structure* (Norman, Oklahoma: Battenburg Press).

Traugott, Elizabeth C. and Pratt, Mary L., 1980, *Linguistics for Students of Literature* (New York: Harcourt Brace Jovanovich).

Trowell, Brian, 1963, 'The Early Renaissance', in Alex Robertson and Denis Stevens (eds), *The Pelican History of Music*, II (Harmondsworth: Penguin).

Tzara, Tristan, 1931, 'Essai sur la situation de la poésie', *Le Surréalisme au Service de la Révolution*, 4, 16–23.

Wellek, René and Warren, Austin, 1963, *Theory of Literature* (Harmondsworth: Penguin).

Westlake, Michael, 1980, *One Zero and the Night Controller* (London: Routledge & Kegan Paul).

Weston, Jessie L., 1957, *From Ritual to Romance* (New York: Doubleday).

Widdowson, H. G., 1975, *Stylistics and the Teaching of Literature* (London: Longman).

Wimsatt, W. K. Jr, 1970, *The Verbal Icon: Studies in the Meaning of Poetry* (London: Methuen).

Winters, Yvor, 1960, *In Defense of Reason* (London: Routledge & Kegan Paul).

Wittgenstein, Ludwig, 1961, *Tractatus Logico-Philosophicus*, tr. D. F. Pears and B. F. McGuinness (London: Routledge & Kegan Paul).

Woodring, C. R., 1968, *Wordsworth* (Cambridge, Mass.: Harvard University Press).

Wordsworth, William, 1947, *The Poetical Works*, ed. E. de Selincourt and Helen Darbishire, 5 vols (London: Oxford University Press).

—— 1965, 'Preface' (1802), *Lyrical Ballads*, ed. R. L. Brett and A. R. Jones (London: Methuen).

Wyatt, Thomas, 1949, *Collected Poems*, ed. Kenneth Muir (London: Routledge & Kegan Paul).

Yeats, W. B., 1961, 'A general introduction to my work', *Essays and Introductions* (London: Macmillan).

Young, Robert, 1979 'A Lacanian reading of Wordsworth's "Prelude"', *Oxford Literary Review*, 3(3), 78–98.

Further reading

Poetry as Discourse has applied to poetry a theoretical approach very close to that put forward by Catherine Belsey in a companion volume in the 'New Accents' series, *Critical Practice* (London: Methuen, 1980). The 'Notes on Further Reading' there give a good list for reading in the linguistics of Saussure and Benveniste, the concept of ideology in Althusser and after, and the psychoanalytic theory of Lacan. There are a lot of books on poetry and poets, probably too many. It would not be hard to give several dozen titles for each of the topics I've written about (metre, the ballad, Shakespeare's sonnets, the poetry of Pope, Wordsworth, Eliot and Pound). Instead, I shall suggest a very small number from which the reader can pick up the trail that interests him or her.

The titles all relate to the idea of poetry as discourse because they all cover general topics or historical periods, not single authors. In the first section I have included essays from the Russian Formalist tradition since they have poetry as a main concern. The second section lists 'classic' literary criticism (as well as Christopher Caudwell), and the third offers some books which have moved beyond traditional criticism in different ways. The fourth section ('Studies in Discourse') is for work on poetry within a perspective similar to that adopted in *Poetry as Discourse*. So far there is very little specifically on poetry to put here, so I have added other works which develop a comparable approach in relation to the novel, the cinema, and 'official' discourse. The final section adds suggestions for the study of music.

1 Linguistics and general

Attridge, Derek, *The Rhythms of English Poetry* (London: Longman, 1982).

Crystal, David, 'Intonation and metrical theory' (*The English Tone of Voice*, London: Edward Arnold, 1975).

Eichenbaum, Boris, 'The theory of the "Formal Method"', in Lee T. Lemon and Marion J. Reis (eds), *Russian Formalist Criticism: Four Essays* (Lincoln: University of Nebraska Press, 1965).

Finnegan, Ruth, *Oral Poetry* (Cambridge: Cambridge University Press, 1977).

Jakobson, Roman, 'The Dominant' in L. Matejka and K. Pomorska (eds), *Readings in Russian Poetics*, (Cambridge, Mass.: MIT Press, 1971).

—— 'Concluding statement: linguistics and poetics', in T. A. Sebeok (ed.), *Style in Language* (Cambridge, Mass.: MIT Press, 1960).

Leech, Geoffrey, *A Linguistic Guide to English Poetry* (London: Longman, 1969).

Mukařovský, Jan, 'Standard language and poetic language', in Paul L. Garvin (ed.), *A Prague School Reader* (Washington DC: Georgetown University Press, 1964).

Shklovsky, Victor, 'Art as technique', in Lee T. Lemon and Marion J. Reis (eds), *Russian Formalist Criticism: Four Essays*, (Lincoln: University of Nebraska Press, 1965).

Traugott, Elizabeth C. and Pratt, Mary L., *Linguistics for Students of Literature* (New York: Harcourt Brace Jovanovich, 1980).

2 Traditional literary criticism

Caudwell, Christopher, *Illusion and Reality, A Study of the Sources of Poetry* (London: Lawrence & Wishart, 1946).

Davie, Donald, *Articulate Energy, An Inquiry into the Syntax of English Poetry* (London: Routledge & Kegan Paul, 1976).

Empson, William, *Seven Types of Ambiguity* (Harmondsworth: Penguin, 1961).

Leavis, F. R., *Revaluation, Tradition and Development in English Poetry* (Harmondsworth: Penguin, 1967).

Nowottny, Winifred, *The Language Poets Use* (London: Athlone Press, 1965).

Wimsatt, W. K. Jr, *The Verbal Icon, Studies in the Meaning of Poetry* (London: Methuen, 1970).

3 Recent criticism

Bloom, Harold, *Poetry and Repression* (New Haven: Yale University Press, 1976).

Cluysenaar, Anne, *Introduction to Literary Stylistics, A Discussion of Dominant Structures in Verse and Prose* (London: Batsford, 1976).
Fish, Stanley E., *Self-Consuming Artefacts: the Experience of Seventeenth-Century Literature* (Berkeley: University of California Press, 1974).
Forrest-Thomson, Veronica, *Poetic Artifice, A Theory of Twentieth-Century Poetry* (Manchester: Manchester University Press, 1978).
Smith, Barbara Herrnstein, *Poetic Closure: A Study of How Poems End* (Chicago: University of Chicago Press, 1968).
Riddel, Joseph, 'Decentering the image: the "project" of "American" poetics?', in *Josué V. Harari* (ed.), *Textual Strategies: Perspectives in Post-Structuralist Criticism* (London: Methuen, 1979).
Riffaterre, Michael, *Semiotics of Poetry* (London: Methuen, 1980).

4 Studies in discourse

Barthes, Roland, *S/Z*, tr. Richard Miller (London: Cape, 1975; a study of a short story by Balzac).
Burton, Frank, and Carlen, Pat, *Official Discourse: On Discourse analysis, government publications, ideology and the state* (London: Routledge & Kegan Paul. 1979).
Durant, Alan, *Ezra Pound, Identity in Crisis* (Brighton: Harvester, 1981).
Ellman, Maud, 'Floating the Pound: the circulation of the subject of "The Cantos"' (*Oxford Literary Review*, 3(3) (1979), 16–27).
Heath, Stephen, 'Narrative space', *Questions of Cinema* (London: Macmillan, 1981).
Kristeva, Julia, *La Révolution du langage poétique: L'Avant-garde à la fin du dix-neuvième siècle; Lautréamont et Mallarmé* (Paris: Éditions du Seuil, 1974).
MacCabe, Colin, *James Joyce and the Revolution of the Word* (London: Macmillan, 1978).
——(book on Milton – forthcoming)
Young, Robert, 'A Lacanian reading of Wordsworth's "Prelude"', *Oxford Literary Review*, 3(3) (1979) 78–98.

5 Music as discourse

The harmonic system of Western music may well be susceptible to the kind of analysis given here to poetry, an analysis which would show that this harmonic system is a bourgeois form. Though claiming to derive naturally from acoustic reality, the Western idiom may in fact be no less conventional – and ideological – than other systems based on different intervals (the medieval modes, the Indian raga). Like iambic pentameter, the harmonic system was developed at the Renaissance and stayed dominant until challenged in this century by (for example) atonal and serialist forms. It certainly invites question. Is melody syntagmatic – and intonational? And so is harmony paradigmatic? What position for the subject is offered by the harmonic system? Someone interested – and competent in music – could start by reading:

T. W. Adorno, *Philosophy of Modern Music*, tr. A. G. Mitchell and W. V. Bloomster (London: Sheed & Ward, 1973).

Chanan, Michael, 'The trajectory of Western music' (*Media, Culture and Society* 3, (July 1970), 219–42).

Middleton, Richard, '"Reading" popular music', *U203 Popular Culture* (Unit 16 (Milton Keynes: Open University Press, 1981).

Index